WHAT LAW RULES?

DAVID A. DWYER

Nancy &
Luther

Wishing you
Both the Best
of All Good
Things

D

WHAT

LAW

RULES?

DAVID A. DWYER

KarDee Libros Ltd.

Published in the United States by
KarDee Libros Ltd.

Cover design by Michael Frank and Dee Dee Jepsen

Printed in the United States of America by
Serbin Printing, Inc. ~ Sarasota, Florida

ISBN
9 780615 421568

First Printing
November, 2010

WHAT LAW RULES?

By
David A. Dwyer

Amen

Nature & the tolls of time – impaired vision – no penalty, no pain – just what fate ordains then offers no compensation. "National Library Services for the Blind" and "National Federation" not empty phrases but escape from empty life, "Talking Book Topics" and "NFB News Line" – that open doors. May all good things happen and all blessings shine on all those who made it happen and those who make it work.

Let this text in intent and spirit so reflect.

TABLE OF CONTENTS

FOREWORD

Who does not want to be exceptional?
Everyone can become an American –
but not every place can become America.

Spanish emigration preceded British and French exploration of the Americas by a hundred years. Their passage via the south Atlantic veered constantly southward and pursued a colonization distinctly theirs.

Adventurers from Northern Europe had braved the rough North Atlantic and then returned, only to go back again, the abundance of America was yet unknown. A century of conflict had drained the treasures of both France and England, a lull in hostilities renewed ambitions to expand. French enterprise was less organized but far more aggressive. Trading Posts had been functioning along the river they had named St. Lawrence and cordial relationships established with Indian tribes.

British structured colonies of distinct regional cultures, differing religious sects, and were forming along the Atlantic coastal regions. These colonies had much in common but took pains to be geographically apart. The staunch Puritans from the mid-land settled in New England; the Quakers from the north of England settled in the valleys south of New York. The aristocratic sons of indulging merchants in the south of England settled in Virginia. All experienced a common transformation as they crossed an angry sea then faced the constant lure of open land that was farther than could be seen. Class-conscious differential immigrants became assertive, Egalitarian Americans. Positive attitudes prevailed as populations grew and cultures blended. What the colonists brought to the wilderness was as important as what they found there.

These first settlers created the unique pride and principles of individual independence and gave substance to the exceptional culture that is the bedrock of the nation. These principles took on legal form with the Declaration of Independence. The exceptional America is primarily cultural then Constitutional:

When in the course of human events it becomes
necessary for one people . . .
to assume among the powers of the earth,
the separate and equal station to which the
Laws of Nature
and Nature's God entitle them.

We hold these truths to be self-evident,
that all men are created equal,
that they are endowed by their Creator with
certain unalienable Rights,
And for the support of this Declaration,
with a firm reliance on the protection of
Divine Providence, we mutually pledge to each
other our Lives, our Fortunes and our sacred Honor.

"We the People" of the of the United States,
in order to form a more perfect Union,
do ordain and establish this Constitution for
the United States of America.

The haunting challenge of the thousands sacrificed, the emotions of remorse, then suppressed but to be forever felt:

…testing if this Nation or any Nation so conceived and
so dedicated can long endure

…that this Nation under God shall have a new birth
of freedom that government of the people, by the people,
for the people shall not perish…

The Nation purged of wrong, the post-war trauma gave way to the aurora of victory in the short Spanish War. A great power now fell prey to ambitions bred within. The lust for glory in a collective rule, the dominance of an anointed few to dispense all rights to their inferiors it was abuses of such rule that has been for centuries the curse throughout crumbling Europe. The equal rights of all men confiscated to serve the greed of few.

The Progressive Movement, an ideology of deceit, and the Constitution cannot live as neighbors. Only one can survive – the one that is best defended.

A Leader Must Arise.

Look in the next mirror –

That Leader could be You!

ACKNOWLEDGMENTS

All formatting and pictorial here credits daughter Dee Dee her talents and graphing skills. All grammar faults are mine alone.

My little sister Claire – we slugged it out together in the tough days.

My nephew Bob Strieder – kindred spirits – never far away.

"Wink" – a stranger who came beside me and changed the odds, during a melee, from three on one. Maybe ten times in the next thirty years "Wink" spotted me and always yelled "Hey, College Boy!" I gladly met him half way. We would just shake hands and trade punches on the arm. We never had anything to say, but he was a friend to whom I still owe a lot.

Gene Kunznick – he paved the way for a law school dropout invading the mystic world of lift, drag and weight control.

Armed Services Procurement Regulations and Certificates of Current Detail: Al Smith, David Meyer and Charles Gaskell – we all served our time there.

Joe Gallagher and Al Ekwald – "Foes" – and respected friends.

Recuerdo siempre los compadres de otros días: concuñado Carlos Malatesta, engineer Walter Hofer, Luís Uchulla, doctores Pedro Moyano y Aurelio Garcia-Sayan, los Fusters, guardaos civil y asaltó – te afeito el culo y protectoras de mi vida.

THE REALITY

Blessings can be tangible, two daughters always made it all worthwhile – time and distance intervenes, yet all things closer – they still inspire…

1941

Karen

2009

Autumn Rain*

Do not stand at my grave and weep;
I am not there.
I do not sleep.
I am a thousand winds that blow.
I am the diamonds gilt on snow.
I am the sunlight on ripened grain.
I am the gentle autumn's rain.
When you awaken in the morning's hush,
I am the swift uplifting rush.
Of quiet birds in circled flight.
I am the soft stars that shine at night.
Do not stand at my grave and cry;
I *am* not there.
I *did* not die.

Thank God for Two Little Girls!

CHAPTER ONE

WHEN LIFE BEGAN AND WHERE

It was Olive Street Road where I lived that was such a dividing line. My family lived to the north on the "have not" side of the road. We happened to be Catholic so the local parish was the social headquarters; economic divisions were in subtle practice. I attended the parish school.

Altar boys were the proud product of the nuns who only tolerated the authority posed by the parish priests. As a nine-year-old altar boy, I was the pride of the parish nuns. The local university language professor in the presence of the pastor had complimented my memory and diction in the audible Latin responses in a Requiem Mass he had attended. I was now the "Icon" of the nuns but the target of the clergy.

Context demands that my acumen be credited to association with my older brother who had been awarded a high school scholarship to a high-track Jesuit Institution. He was the all-time favorite, athletic, a motivated student well tutored by the senior nuns. He had priestly ambitions, I had learned the Latin prayers as his acolyte while he practiced saying Mass. My learning was more by association than his purposeful teaching or my intent.

My addiction to number shortcuts in appreciation of the public library was again formed in following him. My book tastes were in "The Tom Swift Adventures" but I was more exposed to commerce as the politics of the day – I remain committed to the topic. My brother read only books of his interest, which best defines our things in common.

Families of a priest in view expected that other sons would be of opposite bent. Some in my neighborhood prayed that I would atone the evils that must be mine – I was no one's favorite where I lived but I knew I was loved at home.

Altar boy meetings and mass assignments were made by the, prestige hungry, second Associate Pastor. Naturally, to him, Zito Baggleo, recently arrived from Italy, and I, served early morning masses and all funerals of the humble. The English language was new to Zito but Italian was closer to Latin so the two of us in harmony sounded better than the priests.

Only a few people attended the weekday six o'clock morning mass. I quickly learned to recognize anyone who attended several times. My mother and a couple of other ladies were the only ones at mass more than once a week. I came to mass with my mother but I had to put out the candles and get things ready for the next mass. Mom would have left for home before I finished.

It was a Friday – a lady whom I had noticed a few times in the last month or so was waiting as I was leaving church. She was holding a loaded *Saturday Evening Post* sack. Older kids had bags like that over their shoulder delivering magazines. I wanted to get a job there in a couple of years. She asked if I would drop off the packages in the sack at a neighbor's house, as she had to go to the hospital. She also asked if I could help her out next week as the packages were medicine and the people were too sick to get out and get it for themselves. She gave me the addresses – they were all in the neighborhood and on my way home. There were four packages, all bottles wrapped in newspaper. The sack was heavy at first but I felt big with it strapped on my shoulder.

The next week she was waiting for me with another sack every day but Tuesday. She told me how good I was by helping sick people. Friday she told me how well I was doing and she wanted to have me help regularly. She gave me fifty cents and said I would have a job at fifty cents every other Friday. One guy had given me a nickel and I had bought a candy bar with it earlier in the week. I had fifty cents and a regular job.

I was positive my mother would be proud of me, but she wasn't, when I told her about the job. She told me that if any neighbor was sick and I could help them that was what I was supposed to do. The only pay that I could accept was the word "Thanks." She took me back to church. We put the fifty cents in St. Anthony's Box for the poor, and then we went inside and said the rosary. My mother waited for me after mass the following Monday. I saw the lady leaving in her car, she never came back. I had the empty *Saturday Evening Post* sack that I had always given back as I got a new one filled with the packages.

The Gods of Fate may control, but in the world of ten-year-old altar boys, other forces rule. It was just another mass assignment meeting, the associate got to the six o'clock and once again, I won, but before he mentioned Zito, he slurred something about Zito's English. When I asked the associate if he could appoint Zito in Italian – before he could show anger, a fellow altar boy jumped up asking, "Why don't I ever get a chance to serve the six?" Marty who was sitting next to him said "Me too!" Challenged now by two guys from families not to be offended – he mumbled something about a "Sick Call" and that we should continue present assignments. Now red faced, he hurried out the side door. Zito with his head held high went out the front door.

Roman, Marty and I became an inseparable trio as months went by, all good students and generally the class leaders. They lived about two blocks apart but far from my house so we shared time together in their neighborhood, never in mine. They lived in big houses, I did not – their dads were rich, mine was not – nobody cared.

Marty's dad was very strict; he always wore a suit coat or a velvet jacket when at home. Roman's dad was casual; he often wore a sweater and had suit coats with different pants. Both dads were main-aisle ushers at the late Sunday mass. Each then wore navy blue double-breasted suit and light blue ties. I do not think they ever saw one another outside the Church. All three mothers met in the Ladies Sodality; they were all happy with our friendships but had no further association.

It had taken forever but now it felt too soon – the last term in grade eight and high school threatened when it used to be dream. Final exams were over; Mother Superior polled the class to announce their plans for high school. She had three slots for Catholic High for girls and four slots for the school for boys. The rich kids were all giving the schools, Marty had been the first and he gave the name of a strange school but Mother Superior did not pause. She called Roman and he surprised everyone asking for one of the slots at Catholic High; she called my name and I said Public High. She dropped her pen, and then said, "Your mother and I think differently!" The session ended before I had a chance to ask Marty where the school he picked was. Roman came charging up and grabbed my arm, "You pull crap like that again and I'll kick your ass." Marty interrupted, "Mother wants you two to come for lunch, we have something to tell you." We were silent on the short walk to his house.

The table was set for three, a platter of sandwiches and bottles of Coke. Marty's mother handed me a large box from the department store. "Your mother told me she had not had time to get your graduation suit so we agreed that we would be proud if you had the one I got for Marty. He will not be there. Marty has decided to become a priest. He leaves tonight. He will be cloistered in the seminary for the next year and he wanted to share this last afternoon with you two." She left the room, she was not sad – but she was not laughing either.

Marty broke the spell, "It is a good thing that there will be no girls at Catholic High with you two there." We talked too loud and laughed too much. We were too big to cry. It was getting late. Suddenly Marty told me his bicycle was parked on the driveway. Would I take care if it for him? We both knew he would never need it. He punched me on the arm. I could only punch him back. Roman gave him a hug – I wish I had too. Then he was gone. He was smiling – like always. We all wanted to cry.

We knew his mother did not want to say good-bye and

we had nothing left to say. I rode home with the suit box on the handlebars; it was getting dark and so were my thoughts. The three of us now knew separation but we were bonded kindred spirits and would remain as such until the day we die.

I grew up that night, or things grew up around me. All were branded by where they lived. My neighborhood was not the better, but I had friends who lived the better way. No one else knew both sides so well. I had not planned to challenge. Two fellow altar boys – I hardly know from where – my instant allies came. My life now on a different path, I did not know it then – my neighborhood was just left behind. I tried on Marty's suit, it fit me well; there were also three shirts and two striped ties. I felt different. I belonged. It was not just Marty's suit – it was Me!

The Associate Pastor was hated as only a ten-year-old can hate but he was only one. More important were the numbers of other people, they were all proud of where they lived. Some were mean no matter where they lived. I thought it was all the same, it just mattered where your friends were.

Summer was the last of the carefree days. A neighbor of Roman's had graduated from one of the better prep schools and had been accepted at Dartmouth, an Eastern college. He was a football powerhouse – considered a high school standout and well coached. He was working hard to be in condition when school started and invited us to practice with him. Punting was his specialty but strength building was part of the routine. He would kick the ball to me at the end of the field. I would kick it back to Roman about half-way down the field and Roman would pass it on to him. He explained the science involved concerning your foot meeting the ball at just the right spot, and how to swing your leg. "Be sure to keep your eye on the ball." He said I would learn more about this when I studied physics in high school.

Roman was more interested in strength building. By the end of summer Roman was not the middleman, I would catch Jim's punt, run up a few yards and kick it back to him. Jim was impressed. We all said we would do this again next year.

Things occur in series; a neighbor of Roman's stopped

us as we were passing his house. He said he was in the delivery business and needed help for a couple of hours every Wednesday; it was a secret job right in the neighborhood. Roman, my first business teacher, told him that he worked for me and that our fee was five dollars for five hours. He quickly said OK, two dollars every Wednesday for the six stops, do it as quickly as you can. We went to his house on Wednesday night, he gave us a burlap sack, he said the paper-wrapped medicine bottles were to be delivered to the six addresses on the list he gave us along with our two-dollar fee. It took us less than half an hour. One guy gave me a quarter and said something about Canadian; I didn't know what he was talking about so I just said thanks.

Roman told me his father had found out about the venture and that he was furious with the neighbor. I had kept the two dollars so Roman told him he had not gotten any money. From then on, the neighbor did not look at us and we had no reason to look at him.

Bootlegging was not taught in any school – maybe it should have been. A competitive but illegal cottage industry flourished in everybody's town. Treasured recipes were brewed and bottled in family basements by otherwise good law-abiding folks. Delivery was the problem; thirsty clients could not line up at the front door and pay for a package in the view of all to see.

Distribution as a problem was no challenge – a passive public did not care. "Good" citizens were in contempt of a law that said they could not have something that they rarely wanted before there was a law to forbid it.

Hard liquor, smuggled from abroad or distilled in a rural cave the day before, was stored in a well- guarded vacant store; a would-be gangster would only be a nod away. Bonded whiskey was the preference of the affluent. Home delivery was demanded and included in the price. Would-be gangsters were paid for the delivery, the risk, and then belonged to someone else.

Revenuers, aware that delivery was a convenient target, concentrated most of their enforcement effort there. Tragic circumstance can force actions that betray all conscience but reality leaves no choice. A desperate mother, with her baby still at home, pushed the baby carriage delivering bottled booze. There was food that night for the baby safe at home. A prison housed a desperate man who had risked and failed. Life in jail was worse than the Hobo Camps but he would take that risk again – just to shout "No damn surrender! I am a man!" Can right or wrong be rightly judged in the life of someone else?

CHAPTER TWO

HIGH SCHOOL HERO

It was the first day of high school. Roman and I rode the bus to Catholic High. This would be the last time we would be together at the school. We were assigned to different freshmen classes. The first day we got our class schedules and a list of the books we had to buy. We would go to different rooms for every class. The rest of the day the Brothers all told us how tough school would be and that only about half of us would graduate; only some of us would even make it to be sophomores next year. There was a notice on the bulletin board "Football Try-outs" were to be held the next day after class. I met Roman at the try-outs. We were directed to form lines in the spaces that had been assigned – freshmen to seniors.

Brother Vincent said, "The Fathers' Club has provided thirty-five new jerseys. Therefore, the squad this year will be limited. There will be twenty returning from last year's team, other upper class men should forget it. Ten jerseys are reserved for any senior who wants to be on the team for their final year. Should there be a game where we have a big lead in the last minutes, you may get in for a token appearance, but there is no guaranty. The following freshmen are on the team." He called Roman's name. The civilian coach had just stood there looking bored.

When I got home that afternoon, my mom told me that Mother Superior, who had been opposed when I had picked Public High, had seen our mothers at the Sodality meeting.

She had remarked that Mother Superior would like to talk to Roman and me. We arrived at the convent later that day. Mother Superior answered the door herself – she was expecting us. She handed each of us a piece of paper explaining that she had gotten the copies by accident. She directed us to read both sheets. She wanted us to be aware of their contents before she destroyed them.

The Associate Pastor had completed rating forms as requested from Catholic High for all incoming students:

> "Roman: *Affluent family, father active, generous supporter, born leader, good student."*
> "David: *Very modest family, father in ill health, average student, disruptive."*

She was tearing sheets as she closed the door. Roman said, "I wonder if Public High had forms like that? Hey, how did I make the team when nobody saw me play?"

Freshman year was not a happy time.

I was maybe the average thirteen-year-old, lucky enough to be a high school sophomore. Some guys I knew in grade school were now in jail. I attended Catholic High, but never really belonged – an "Under Achiever" was the faculty view. College prep schools were the interest of this religious order. The faculty at Catholic High was some twenty brothers, their opinion of my aptitude and attitude was divided. It was deserved. I had yet to realize that the term "smart ass" is in error – the word "smart" is out of place. To be fair – certain of the teaching brotherhood, too, bore guilt.

I rode Marty's bike to school in good weather but I had to make other plans for rain and snow. I found a partner "Phil." Kids who lived on the south side and didn't need a second bus would ask for a transfer and then give it to Phil. He would pass them to me through the bus window. I had a group of kids who lived west. There was a westbound bus line on the next corner.

The kids were glad to buy a transfer for half the bus fare. Phil and I would split fifty cents on most days.

Roman discovered girls about sixty minutes before I did. He suddenly became aware of a girl that had always lived across the street, or maybe she became aware of him. Her name was Peggy. She was the "Salome" of the time; Roman was the "Lothario" of the day. She was a neighbor; they had played together when they were kids. She was sitting on her front porch and she was no longer a kid.

He dragged me over to her saying I want you to meet the "Pride of Catholic High." She turned, as only she could turn, and put out her hand to shake mine saying "Hello Roman. I am glad to meet your friend. You should both stop by when you have time. Peggy looked like a movie queen and Roman was in her plans. Fate may control, but Peggy was always there to help. It was in the Stars – Peggy also had a friend, her name was Hope – life would never be the same.

It was maybe one hour later that same Saturday; we were throwing a baseball back and forth when Peggy and a friend just happened to be riding by on their bicycles. They stopped to watch. Peggy and her friend both had ponytails and wore skirts that looked like trousers. I had already lost my heart to Peggy's friend who was smiling just at me. Her name was Hope. That was all I heard as Peggy was telling her I was the "Pride of Catholic High."

Somehow, we were now down the street at Peggy's house sitting on the patio looking out at her tennis court. I saw four bicycles on the driveway so we must have all ridden there.

I was tongue-tied as Hope was looking at me asking about Catholic High; she had not heard of it before. Roman was quick, "We all speak Latin there so it is very secret and too hard to explain." She was very impressed. She asked me to say something in Latin. I rattled off "Ora pro nobis" and she was in awe. My confidence returned.

Things settled down. Roman and Peggy were fascinating each other on the tennis court. Hope was telling me about the academy she attended, and that she was having trouble with

Algebra. She was having difficulty understanding how numbers could become letters. Naturally, I began to explain it. She said, "You make it so easy! Can we go to my house so I can get the book and you can show me?" Peggy waved telling Hope to call her that night; Roman just gave me the high sign.

She got the book and we went to what she called the gazebo. We were busy with Algebra when her mother drove up the drive and stopped when she saw us studying. She was friendly, remarked how studying was time well spent and went inside. Hope was learning fast. She corrected me: if A+B=32 then B=17 if A=15 not 13 as I had said. My mind had not been on Algebra, but I must be a good teacher.

I was shooting baskets in Roman's driveway a few days later. We had intended to "just happen to pass" Peggy's house; I knew Hope was there. Just as Roman came out to join me, the mayor who lived next door came over. He was a close friend of Roman's dad and asked to talk to me. I was flattered that the mayor would want to talk to me, but Roman was not surprised. The ambitious city mayor, predicted to be the next governor, was publicly proclaimed the "Patron of the Boy Scouts." He was everybody's hero. He wanted my advice! The girls would be impressed.

The mayor was real. He was anxious to get a lot of votes from my neighborhood in the coming election. He had not done well there in the past. He also wanted to advertise the Boy Scouts. Would I join his troop? Roman was already a member. I could pick up my uniform at the department store. I would repay the troop with good deeds.

The idea was that Roman and I, two neatly uniformed boy scouts, would pass out his election cards outside churches. It would help his election and help the scouts. Who could refuse to do good twice?

We did our thing well. We were outside every church in town at least three times. We were popular, always smiling and always courteous – that is what the *Morning Globe* reported but they did not put in the picture they took at the Cathedral.

The mayor won, it was a landslide. He got eighty

percent of my neighbor's votes. My career was launched, politics committed, support not yet consigned. The Mayor honored us at the Victory Party. He presented us with a gift certificate for the Hangout High. Ten bucks does not go far when you are standing root beer floats for everybody there.

When we were leaving the Hangout, a well-dressed guy caught up with us. He had heard good things about us. His company was interested in a uniformed delivery service – twenty small packages, all-local addresses, five bucks each, Thursday night after dark, should take about two hours. Nothing to debate – twenty packages – two hours – five bucks. "Where do we meet you Thursday after dark?" Roman grabbed the card he was handing me. "Be on time! Wear your Scout uniform!" He snarled, then was gone.

The address was in a tough district, but we were not going to move there. It was a darkened storefront. The door opened before I knocked. There were two official Scout knapsacks filled with packages wrapped in newspaper. A different guy handed me a list. He also gave a five-dollar bill to each of us. This was the first time I had five dollars in my hand that was at least part mine.

"This is a list of addresses. You don't need to know the names. Make the deliveries and go home. Don't come here. We'll contact you at the High School Hangout."

We were on our way; the addresses were all in good areas not too far apart. There were twenty-three packages, not the agreed-upon twenty but who counts at five bucks for two hours. We were about half-way through before we admitted to each other that we had been cheated once. So what was next? All the packages were bottles. We got the job because nobody questioned a Boy Scout doing a good deed. Greed had wings and we were stupid!

Delivery service was not for us. We delivered the rest, twenty-three not twenty, fifteen percent more then we agreed to deliver, but we gained a buck fifty in tips. The lesson was worth far more than that; morality claims a higher fee. Roman would not take any of the money. He rattled on that it was all my lousy idea. It was a good thing that he had able to save my butt again. We both knew he did it just to help me out, but it sounded good at the time.

I gave my mother five bucks saying I had been paid for political work. Then three bucks to the troop to pay for the uniform. I had failed good deeds.

I bought a used two-speed Racer bike, for two bucks it would be easier to pump the distance to school. There must have been a message – the bicycle was stolen the next Sunday. I had parked it in front of church while I was at mass. I never tried to get it back.

That creep was outside the Hangout the following week. I spit on the sidewalk when he looked at me as I walked inside – Roman had been looking out the window, he punched me on the arm. We never talked about it.

Roman's roving eye was leading him down new paths. He was becoming more involved at school and I had a transfer exchange enterprise to take care of, so we only got together on the weekends. There was no fire in hell that could ever warp our kindred spirits but diverging interests can divide.

We had been busy getting the Mayor elected so he had not had seen Peggy but they had been talking on the phone. Hope had invited us for tennis this Saturday. I was still in awe; I had not been in contact with Hope for a while. Roman and Peggy wanted to play tennis. Hope and I wandered back to the gazebo – better to be alone; study not in mind.

Hope's mother was friendlier; she thought it was fine that we were studying together. Hope's father was pleased that she was continuing Algebra and that she invited me. Hope had gotten an A+ in Algebra last year. It was taught in the eighth grade at her school. I was surprised. Algebra was discussed again, but we also found other things to talk about. I was invited to drop by the following Wednesday – "If I had the time."

Ted Scott was a transfer client, his family had recently moved into the area so we had ridden the bus together in bad weather. His bus stop was after mine so I never knew where he lived. I was peddling my bike along that Wednesday, a couple of blocks from Hope's house, when Ted yelled at me. He lived just across the street from Jim Dugan, my kicking coach. Ted and I had mutual interests; we were to become fast friends.

Hope went to an all-girls' academy. She would be taking the next semester in France. Hope had been studying French for two years. She expected to be fluent in French when she entered college. Her parents were hosting a picnic mixer the next Saturday and her mother had suggested that she invite me. We would leave from her house about noon. Could I come? I was saying "Sure" before she said it all.

The picnic was different; nobody brought baked beans and potato salad from home. It was held at an elaborate patio with a large brick fireplace on the campus of Hope's school. No one had to cook their hot dog on a stick over the open fire. Two men in big white hats were cooking. It looked like ribs in the fireplace and there was a big ham. There was a big round table with a tablecloth and eight chairs for the parents. Two ladies waited on them. They were drinking wine. The kids served themselves; there were white picnic tables and pitchers of lemonade. You just sat at any vacant table. Everyone was friendly, just having fun. The parents played bridge after lunch. Rosita, a friend of Hope's, joined us. She was from New Jersey, and a resident at the academy. Rosita did not have a date. She thought local boys were creeps but said I was different.

We walked around; the academy went from seventh grade through high school. There were eighty-one pupils; sixty-five were residents mainly from the East. Rosita said her father wanted her to see how people lived west of Niagara Falls. We passed the tables where the parents were playing bridge.

Rosita told us she had been playing bridge since she was a little girl. She was practiced with the Culbertson system and all the bidding signals. She would teach us but we would need a fourth player. I knew Roman would not be interested but I thought Ted would. Ted could change her mind about local men. Rosita would spend some welcomed time with Hope and the three of us would master bridge. It became a regular Saturday date but all too soon, June came.

A happy time was ending. Rosita was now leaving for home and Hope was going to leave for France in August. Roman's family went on a cruise and Peggy had been enrolled in some kind of a culture camp during the summer of 1933. She was enthusiastic about grand opera and the ballet. Jim Dugan was back. Ted Scott joined Jim and me in our workouts.

The sophomore year allowed, but now is only history.

Ted and I spent quite a bit of idle time together. I was welcomed in his family circle. Ted's father was an engineer and had a terrific sense of humor. He had invented some kind of a rifle. It was very popular in Europe due to the War in Spain. The U. S. Army was now very interested in it. Ted's mother was also an engineer; their friends were all engineers or professors.

Ted's sister Virginia was a world apart. She was not the typical female student at a college where girls went to study, not to meet men. She was majoring in history at Washington University. She was good looking, intelligent and she knew it. Open flirting was her pastime and she just kept in practice tempting me. I was in awe of her. She told me I was clumsy, needed a haircut and was too cute to have been an altar boy. She advised that I had better learn how to dance if I wanted to appeal to that girl up the street.

She would try to teach me if I washed her car. I thanked her for the offer but I was an excellent dancer and was busy at football with an All-American from Dartmouth. It was inevitable that she would learn of Coach Jim. I did not tell her he lived across the street and Ted was knew him as well. I retorted, "A would-be nun shouldn't dance and All-Americans don't work out with guys who washed cars."

I did not know how she did it but the next day she was suddenly on the practice field to tell Ted that he was to stop and pick up some eggs. Jim interrupted, "My name is James Dugan. You, Miss, have intruded my session in laboratory physics. Eggs should be kept on ice. Your credentials, please." The flash of attracting sparks, the interchange could be seen a mile away and somewhere thunder rocked as cupids danced. Jim spent more time at the Scotts than I did. Jim left for his final term at Dartmouth. Virginia drove him to the train station, everybody else stayed home.

As a high school junior Hope had left for her semester's study in Paris. Her parents were going to join her in Paris at Christmas. She would be back at the academy for the second semester. Ted had a friend in Public High who told him that outside kids were welcome to sit in classes without being invited. The gym had just been remodeled and was supposed to be the best in the state. The day after Halloween, All Saints Day, was a Catholic holiday so we checked the public high school out. Ted thought the best-looking girls were seniors but he followed the first girl that looked at him. Hope had my interest so I went to an all-male gym class. It was a good thing that I did.

The instructor was also one of the coaches. He was glad to welcome any local who went to another school. He worked for the district so he taught any kid that came. The class that day was touch football: passing, receiving and kicking were the lessons. He was impressed with my kicks. He was sorry I went to Catholic High. A lot of good talent got lost there since they had no organized programs or professional coaches. He encouraged me to come back any time; he mumbled something about wasted talent.

I returned to the gym on Catholic holidays and attended wrestling team practice after school. The coach taught me how to balance and concentrate. His masterstroke was having me entered in the State High School Wrestling Finals. I think it was his gesture of defiance aimed at the Catholic High coaches. I made it to the quarterfinals however; the next-to-be-champion spared my life. He was later disqualified; he was two years over age and had been kicked out of a reform school in Kentucky.

Romance ignores events and time; it is only we that age. Roman's roving eye was not focused. Peggy had more goals in mind, maybe everything in pants. They continued those tempting moves, each just playing games. I was in love with Hope; I think I was her mark as well. Her parents were watching by. I was invited to her home; they made sure I was relaxed.

Her father was impressive; he casually questioned me. Her mother would light up any room; she could charm a snake. I was invited back; talk more open, I began to feel at home. Her father more like a mentor than anyone I had met before, or since; her mother was from another world. I was coolly monitored as if serving her ambitions for her daughter. I was being tutored in the nuance and behavior of the chosen sect.

I willfully embraced this environment of solid comfort with caution, no thought of disappointment but instincts prevail. Hope told me her folks were planning a party for her sixteenth birthday but it was a secret. She didn't know why her father wanted me to pass by his office Friday after class – there must be a connection.

When I arrived there Friday after class, I was asked to wait a bit and was offered a Coke. I do not know why I declined. A buzzer sounded and I was escorted inside. He came right to the point. He had been measured for a tuxedo and the tailor had it all cut and the first fit was perfect but he had been too busy so he had skipped the final fitting; he had paid the tailor. Now it did not fit. He had gained some weight as the doctor said he should. The tailor could make things smaller but no way to alter it larger. The tailor was coming by to measure him again, he was bringing the tuxedo, it might fit me.

The tailor was a classic Italian artisan. He never stopped talking as he slipped the jacket over both arms remarking about my shoulders but he was changing pins and pulling threads and smoothing one place as he punched another and the jacket suddenly felt like my skin and his chatter halted. "You, Sir, a perfect fit," and there was no accent. "There is absolutely no further charge but I want to present you with my best formal shirt and custom tie set if you will pass my business card to your friends and recommend my talents. I want to have more young clients." I owned a tux at age 16! The tailor went on as his helper was measuring the trousers length – "Your formal wear will be available Tuesday noon."

Roman presented me with a pair of patent leather shoes,

a present he had never worn. He thought they were effeminate – they would look good on me.

There was a party like few have ever seen. Hope was a floating cloud, a fairy princess; I was the perfect consort. No one had to tell us how we looked together. Roman had picked me up, tuxedos were not popular where I lived and not intended for a bicycle. He went on to pick up Peggy.

Hope's parents were waiting, the door opened before I rang the bell. I felt they were checking me all over, as they were too casual to be real. Her mother was glowing. For the first time she kissed me on both cheeks. Her father clutched my arm as Hope danced down the stairs. The mood was contagious bejeweled and glamorous ladies, men in black and white. Everyone smiled. There was no outside world for tonight, no trouble seen. Hope's father gave the toast, her mother joined him at the end. I tried not to stare as the crowd sang "Happy Birthday" as they were holding hands – the party was for them.

The mayor, now a candidate for governor, cut in as I was dancing. He said, "Let's chat after this dance." Sure enough, I was having a Coke with Peggy and Roman; they were heading for the dance floor as the mayor sauntered up with another man. We shook hands and the mayor introduced his friend, telling him that I had helped him get elected. A friendly over-statement, it was casual but intended. Could it be my tailor-made tuxedo? Or that I belonged? The chat lasted maybe two minutes but it would be remembered. His friend remarked rather than asked if I was graduating. Not waiting for an answer he handed me a card – "Be sure to contact me when you are out of school next year." They were two tables away before I awakened.

Hope's father insisted on driving me home. Hope and her mother were still entertaining the post-party breakfast. He had left his reserve. He thanked me for being a part of a tradition of importance to his wife and later to Hope. I did not understand but just kept quiet – this was his night. He drove right to my front door without directions; he must have been here before. It could have been the White House, his attitude was the same. He offered his hand – "You did well tonight" – then he was gone. He drove down the street as if it had been driven many times before.

Some nights are just not made for sleep to steal. There was no time to dream – only plans are real. Hope – the mayor/governor – the mayor's friend – tuxedo – graduation – career. Who had been used the more and then used in turn? This front yard, this porch, all that rests inside – Why stare at the moon? I had left it all behind when Hope's mother embraced me. She had found where I belonged, but I had no firm commitment, I had not sold my soul. I had passed all tests – so far.

I learned to think in grade school and I found ways to maneuver, not to just survive. Three years in high school, maybe three bad teachers but any failure was left to me. I had friends, more luck than some – but there were things denied. All things are in balance, opportunity does not await but waits to be found. It is America that is unique! "A Culture." It is people and circumstance that merge. "All Men are Created Equal," that New World awaits but the door slams shut on the unprepared.

CHAPTER THREE

THE NEW DEAL

I would graduate in June the next year – FDR would still have a year to go. He had changed a lot in just two years, but people stayed the same throughout the World. I read the business card I had been given at the party – it was meant to serve me well but at a later time.

"We the People"
not one song but two;

"Happy Days Are Here Again"
The Good Times of Desire

"Buddy Can You Spare a Dime?"
The Testing Times of Hope

As expected, Virginia and Jim announced their engagement. The wedding would be in early June. They both insisted that our age was not significant and that Ted and I were to be part of the wedding party. Two very attractive Washington U. coeds were delighted to entice younger men. The bachelor party, the night before the wedding, was the highlight for Ted and me. Ted was sure we had Cokes while the other twenty guys, all out of college, had booze. They all treated us as if we belonged. Ted and I left just after dinner. The steaks were the thickest and the best that I have ever seen.

Sons of the Opera Board or politicians filled usher jobs at the Muny Opera. Roman's dad had gotten a slot for Roman but he turned it over to me. I was not assigned an aisle but for some reason I got a fancier white uniform and a special cap. Roman's dad must be a big shot. I had a special spot; my job was for the full eight-week season, all others were for just four weeks. People, after coming through the gate, would show me their ticket stub. I would tell them what level to go to and how many aisles to pass on their right or left. Season ticket holders did not pay any attention to me. It was really a simple job. There were only three levels for the four different priced seats and each priced seat ticket had a different color. The ticket had right, left or center section for the three levels printed on them. I had to figure out the aisle by the seat number, so if I had to guess I would pick the middle aisle. I was never more than one aisle off. I never heard of a complaint.

Press people, politicians and some other influential people had unusual tickets. These were for a private parking lot with a private connecting gate to a special box-seat section. The special box seats were nearly filled on weekends. It was only natural that the ushers in charge of this special section would become friendly with some of the ones responsible for the other sections. Professional courtesy prevailed. The parking facility and private gate assignees and their dates enjoyed weekly performances. Every Tuesday Roman, Peggy and Hope were so accommodated throughout the eight-week season. I took off after the first scene, changed out of uniform and joined them for the show.

Art Hill, our local lover's lane, always followed. We would park our car atop a high hill, which overlooked a romantic lake basin glistening in the moonlight. This was the highlight of the evening. I worked five nights a week, but I got off after the first act every other night. Hope and I took long walks
and I had money to afford an occasional stop at the Hangout.

The summer of 1934 is remembered as a carefree, happy time.

Things were evaluated on the average then, what else applies? It was and is a "Culture" unique throughout the world – "We the People" – not by fate but by instinct, we share and guard each other.

Not One Song but Two;

"Buddy Can You Spare a Dime?"
When Things Are Poor

"Happy Days Are Here Again"
When Things Are Well

CHAPTER FOUR

THE ENTREPRENEUR

The Baseball Cardinals had won the pennant, the Gas House Gang was wildly popular and Sportsman Park was sold out. I got a job as an usher at the stadium, so I skipped school for two days during the World Series. I had to report to the ballpark before eight o'clock. They sold standing-room-only tickets, for an hour at noon, to people who had been standing for hours before game time. I had made friends with a fireman who said he was the security officer stationed at my aisle, which was just on the outfield side of third base. He said the ball team was a good friend to cops and firemen. They got a chance to see the game and they had free beer and hot dogs in the guardroom by pulling security duty. The owner thought the crowd might be unruly. He had good things to say about the club owner. It was he who remarked how hot it was going to get and how some guys would like a chance to sit on a vacant step. He left going to the guardroom for a snack – if there was any disturbance for me to look for any cop but him. He would be back at game time.

When he came back, all twenty steps were occupied by happy guys in comfort. The fireman didn't notice, but said he could guard better behind third base and that I could work toward the outfield. Exit via the back gate would be easier to beat the crowd after the game. I watched the game from deep in left field through the eighth inning and was a half mile away on the streetcar before the game was over. I had twenty-four bucks. It was the most money I had ever held.

The next day a surly cop was on my aisle – he didn't even say "hello." My friend the fireman passed by on his way to the guardroom, he casually remarked that the chief usher came by. "I told him you had gone to the can and that you were probably caught up in the crowd." He was fifty feet away before I could say "Thanks."

The chief usher came by. "You are new, but you should have known not to leave the aisle before game time. You should have gotten tips before the steps were grabbed. All tips are turned in to me. I will be by during the seventh inning to collect your tips. The tips will be split after the series. You ushers are lucky to see the game for free!" I replied, "Sure."

The cop had walked down the aisle and was staring at the field. "I'm going for lunch, be sure to keep the aisle clear till I get back." I said, "Sure." When he got back, I had kept half the aisle open. I had learned yesterday that close to game time aisles can be filled fast. I had over thirty bucks. The cop smelled as if he had beer for lunch. He parked himself on a waste bucket that he had found and was taking a nap. I knew the sport was over and quit while I was ahead. I left him to greet the head usher; I took off after the sixth Inning – the Cardinals were ahead.

I gave my mother twenty-five bucks. I knew that she depended on me for things that are more important than money but she had never questioned me before – "This is a lot of money!" I said the Cards did not need any substitutes, so I did not get to play or to get any prize money – I knew she believed what she wanted to believe.

I had forty-seven bucks left. I hid it in a Prince Albert tobacco can and hid the can in the attic. I knew I would need money for graduation; I had outgrown Marty's navy blue but well remembered what the suit had done for me. I was born confident. Now, I was the one to challenge. The World was mine.

I remembered that I had two dollars salary to collect from the Cardinals. I was to be paid at a rate of $1.00 a day. I called the ballpark. A rather unfriendly person answered the phone; I asked if she could mail me my salary. She replied you must be rich; I was about to file the ledger. I gave her my name and she said there is no initial but there is an X behind your name. I guess you cannot write."

"Oh no, I am an honor student at Catholic High," I lied.

"The team can spare a stamp, give me your address. I never saw an honor student and I would like to keep it that way." She replied. Two dollars in a folded sheet of blank paper was in the mail the next day. It was just in time. The bulletin board announced that the invitations and calling cards that every graduate was required to buy were in the principal's office. There was a small box of fifty calling cards and a larger box of ten invitations. The fee was two dollars and had to be paid before diplomas were prepared. I was impressed, maybe proud, when I opened the box of invitations:

"You are cordially invited to attend
Commencement Exercises
The Class of 1935"

The calling cards: my name appeared in bold script on an edged buff card. These cards would be carefully placed in ensuing years to frame a tattered past. I bought a turkey for a Christmas dinner surprise; it was the first turkey dinner I remember.

Christmas 1934 was not a happy time for far too many.

I shopped for my next important graduation suit. I had to match the projection of my tuxedo. Weil Clothing had a window special. Grey plaid for ten bucks but the salesman convinced me that the rack model at twelve bucks would be a better fit and not wrinkle. Boyd's Men Shop and Wolf Haberdashery had far better material and full alterations starting at twenty bucks. I bought a pair of black wing tips at Hanover Shoes for four bucks; McCann's had squared-toe shoes at three fifty but I passed. I had thirty-six bucks left. I settled on a grey flannel at Boyd's for twenty-two bucks. The alterations were perfect and grey flannel reeked good taste, as had my navy blue. I had the striped ties from Marty and I knew I looked great. I was ready to take on the world.

The second semester, mid-term exams had been graded. There were no failures in the class. Graduation plans took over. The class president, not a favorite guy, wanted ten bucks to give a class token gift to Catholic High and he had to reserve a graduation night farewell. I liked the party idea – I was one of the first to commit. I joined Roman in a petition that the class token gift be a bronze tablet of the Eighteenth Amendment.

The petition died but "inventive fantasy" the class of '35 lives on.

Who is to question the whim of the stars? Who has the right to dispute passage, or maybe just to teach some more important things? The principal who had been most fair was transferred to another school – it was May Day 1935. Brother Aloysius, a nemesis for the four years, had an ally and struck a final blow at midnight but other stars converged. One last look behind and a pledge to never look back again.

Commencement: a dull exercise, dull speeches, diplomas were just handed out. The test was to find the guy that got the one with your name on it. The graduation party was the only thing to remember. We doubled with Roman and Peggy and ended up on Art Hill. It was a night of a thousand stars and a million dreams, no groping hands and wild promise but tender kisses and plans.

Hope gave me her class ring.
The only thing I had to give her was my diploma.
It was my pledge, my commitment.

CHAPTER FIVE

MATRICULATE IS JUST A WORD

I was on cloud nine the following day. The coach at Public High had highly recommended me for a St. Louis University Summer Try-out Camp. Catholic High had not responded. Coach Duford was mean enough to be a guard in a Florida chain gang; his two assistant coaches had to prove they were meaner still. A two-week camp split offense and defense two four-hour workouts a day and any position the coach told you to play, you played. The first day of week two – three of us accompanied by three guys to play center were held over for kicking drill. We kicked from the fifty-yard line and the target was a water bucket, two yards from the goal line and on the right or left sideline. We took turns after ten kicks with a different center every turn. I was the only one getting all my kicks inside the ten-yard line. I hit the bucket twice. There were only two of us kicking the second day, one guy played center and the other two played the defensive line. It was a test in blocking and kicking under pressure.

Coach Duford took me over to the bench; he was reading from a clipboard, "A good kicker – more quick than fast, any back on defense – a blocking back or pulling guard." He looked me in the eye; "You have an Alumnus Sponsor. A scholarship is yours, break a rule, or miss in academics and it's yours to lose. A voucher is in the bookstore, you are registered in commerce, get class assignments." He didn't shake hands or smile – I either laughed or cried – I could never remember which.

College Day School lasted just a month, a "shattered bubble" my alumnus patron bought, he should have sold (I still remember him at prayer). The registrar gave me the word there was no one to pay tuition; the books were mine the athletic department had paid for them. I could have left through the crack under the door.

Where do you go? I had been pushed off a cloud – go anywhere – some place – just to start again. Roman was on somebody's yacht somewhere; and Marty far away, would have the known the right words to say. I was alone. It was a long way from commencement. I passed the field where Jim taught me how to kick. What had happened? For what reason? Why? I walked toward Hope's but I knew they were not home. Somebody was walking with me; it was Peggy. We walked on; neither spoke, I knew she belonged. We ended up on the patio, the tennis court close by. Melba the maid, who was more like a protector to both of us, came out with a tray of food and a pot of tea – still hot. "Your Mother is having another tea party and you both look better out here." I knew that life had changed when the registrar wished me well.

Many hours on the tennis court and playing hands and knees on the patio – it had always been Peg and Roman, Hope and me, a closed quartet. She called me Bro, there was no reason why, she never called anyone by name. She was always just Peg to me and others in the know.

CHAPTER SIX

THE BREAKING DAWN

The next morning, the first day of the new fresh start, my suit of armor was flannel grey, my weapons were self-confidence and a packet of calling cards. My assault weapon was the business card of Robert B. Hannigan. I decided to hit there next. His department in the New Federal Building was listed as 1209 through 1221. I entered 1209.

An attractive but very efficient appearing blonde-haired woman sat at a desk, a number of partially occupied straight chairs lined two walls. She asked if I had an appointment, I handed her the card and said Mr. Hannigan told me to see him when I finished school. Reading the card, she dialed the phone and after a short interchange, she directed me to another room where a Mrs. Day would be waiting for me. I was impressed, she smiled but the other people waiting gave me dirty looks.

It was a small outer office, wall-to-wall carpet instead of tile and pictures were on the wall. A sophisticated mid-aged lady, best described as handsome, was seated at a large wooden desk. The polished top was solely occupied by a small crystal vase of roses, probably cut in the early morning from her personally tended garden. One could wager that multi-colored baby mums were featured in a later season.

I offered the card as she went on to explain that he would be in Washington for the immediate future. The middle drawer was being opened slightly and she was checking the card against something in the drawer. Her half smile had remained frozen.

From somewhere she pulled out a small piece of paper and handed it to me. "I'm sure Mr. Hannigan would want to offer assistance. In his absence, Mr. Butler is available. He will join you in the conference room behind us. "Please complete this form pending his arrival,"

I found myself in a leather chair at a small table, not sure how I got there as a well-dressed man was coming through the door she was now closing. I was aware of his careful scrutiny as he engaged me in small talk. He was casual but my stay at St. Louis U. was of most interest. Mr. Butler was overly alert to his own concerns and was careless in concealment. He asked too many off-handed questions as to how close I was to the ambitious mayor.

I started with the Boy Scouts and the handing out of campaign stuff outside churches. The mayor said I had helped him win the Third Ward. I was casual in remarking that we often met at social functions. He interrupted asking, "How many?" I was casual saying I was on the stag list, which was like an invitation to most things, and I dropped Hope's father's name.

"Mr. Hannigan is in Washington working out the details of a program that will fit you, but it will take several weeks to finish. It would be to your advantage to use this time to gain work experience. I will check to see if anything is available."

He returned handing me a form and a return envelope. The Local News Co., Mr. Assi Rogan, and an address were on top, two lines below was printed,

"Introducing: David A. Dwyer"

My name was typed in. "I have just talked to Assi Rogan and he is expecting you this afternoon. You should change clothes; they would not like your suit. Good Luck and I am sure we will meet again." We shook hands. Mrs. Day smiled, said "Good luck, David." She had used my name!

Mr. Rogan was built like a fullback only taller. He had

red hair and did not know how to smile. He took the form and checked off some items before he said a thing.

"Let's see if you can add and multiply," he remarked, as he passed me a stack of about ten six-by-twenty inch yellow sheets marked "Invoice." "Magazine Titles" and "Price" were listed down the left side – a column headed "Quantity" and one headed "Due" with a "Total" on the bottom of the sheet.

There was a box of pencils on the table so I did what I thought was expected. I ripped through the sheets while he stared. When I handed the stack back to him he pushed a button and he gave the stack to a young lady saying, "See how many mistakes you can find."

She was gone but a few minutes; he had stared out the window, so did I. She returned and said, "There were no mistakes, but some numbers were not clear. I thought there were errors but it was his writing, he should use sharp pencils." Mr. Rogan asked me, "How did you know what to do?"

I started to explain, however before I said a word, he stated, "We work as teams. We start at seven-thirty and should quit at five but the day's work has to be done. I don't know anything about overtime and don't care how much time you take for lunch up to half an hour.

"Monday is van deliveries and freight yard pickups. Move the magazines to the top floor, stack them in their places on the tables, and start loading delivery trucks. On Tuesday, the dealers' bins are stuffed. Wednesday and Thursday are delivery and invoicing days. Friday we process the unsold magazines. Drivers give a returned receipt to the dealer and the totals must match the covers that are returned to the publisher. If there is, anything left over from Friday it is made up on Saturday. You can see that everything is checked and balanced; you can have all the magazines you want as long as the covers have been processed. The last guy that thought he could steal from the company ain't here anymore. He probably left town wishing he had been arrested and sent to jail – it would have been easier.

"Your salary is twelve bucks; Saturday is payday. Do you want to start tomorrow or wait for next Monday?"

"I'll take tomorrow if I get the twelve bucks on Saturday, I feel like I worked today" I replied. He stared at me, seemed like forever.

"Yea, but I won't forget you owe me. Fill out this card and leave it at the cash window. Your team-workers won't like you and it's your job to get along with them – be on time!" He left expecting I could find my way out. I filled out the card. Name / Address / Phone / Closest Relative / Last Job / Doctor (Dr. Mudd, I was examined by him for my St. Louis U. physical at St. Mary's Hospital) / Have you ever been in jail?

I was employed! Not then, smart enough to know why or how.

He was right; I was not to be one of the guys. I was early my first career day, the door was still locked. A not-unfriendly guy, he must have been thirty, said, "You're the one! I'm Angelo – I'll tell you what to do." Five others came up together. "Here's Tony, Jasper, Geno, Tony and Sal." The five just raised a hand in turn. It was clear they didn't care who I was.

We were standing in front of a big garage door; the office door was in the middle of the building. Angelo had a key to open the big elevator. Two moving vans rolled in, I guessed on schedule. There were five hand trucks on the elevator. Each man grabbed a hand truck. The magazines were in bundles stacked on pallets. These were soon stacked high aboard the elevator.

Mr. Rogan pulled into a fenced parking lot across the street while this was going on. He didn't say a word and no one paused. It was as though this was the way it was every Monday morning. I busied myself just trying to get out of the way. The two Tonys were now stacking loose bundles along the curb. Mr. Rogan was inspecting the van, I guessed, to be sure it was empty as the second van was attacked. Angelo said, "Come with me."

We got on the elevator as the two Tonys hurriedly also got on with hand trucks and Angelo pulled the gate down. We were on the top floor when Angelo said, "Grab that hand truck in the corner and get with it." I was lucky I slid my truck under a pallet of "Love Stories," a popular pulp, and followed one of the Tonys the short distance to a long table. It was striped across the top with numbers one through five. Between racks of open shelves, it was divided into compartments about two feet square from knee-to-shoulder high. He had "Love Stories" as well, so it was easy.

He wheeled up to space five and unloaded the magazines into the space. I followed, but my next load was "Popular Mechanics" so I started space four as Angelo still watched. After my fourth trip, he said, "Come with me. Lombard, said, you should know about the business." How did I know he meant Mr. Rogan?

"We receive twenty truck deliveries. About ten truckloads deliver cut-bundles. The drivers work out with the little drug stores and newsstands. We charge everything to the drivers and give them a receipt. Full bundles are made up in the bins you just saw. Different month magazines have different dates; we match the week they were issued. Me and the guys do the bin stuff on Tuesdays and part of Wednesday. You give us the invoice to put on top and we take the bundles down to the trucks. You are downstairs checking the drivers until we start packing on Wednesday. Friday and Saturday, we do returns. Lombard checks everything. All magazines are counted, which means your invoices have to be totaled and finished. The girls on the machines get everything checked before we get off, so pay attention." I became aware that "Lombard" had been standing behind me, listening to it all.

Suddenly it was Thursday and all hell broke loose. The count didn't check! A bundle of "Popular Mechanics" was missing and everybody was looking at me. On Friday morning, Sal found the bundle. It was far back on the floor below the bottom bins. Angelo looked at the crew, not at me, "This ain't gon'na help any of ya!"

We all ended up in the basement. The returns were all tied with tough white twisted rope; a return slip in an envelope was on top. The envelope had a number on it in large heavy print; the return slip had the number and account name. The number returned was entered next to the magazine name. The guys all had knife rings on to cut the twisted rope. They gave the envelopes to me and separated the magazines into stacks. They called out the number, which I checked against the slips. They tore the covers off and gave them to Angelo, seated next to me at the head of the table. Pulps were being allowed to stack up in front of me. Their stacks were not in near the quantity as those piled in front of me. They were tearing single copies as they watched me hurt. The return slips were not fresh new paper, easy to handle, but far to the contrary. It took me longer to read them and do the arithmetic.

Did they expect me to tear all the pulps as well? It was getting close to noon. Angelo was too interested in counting covers but I knew he was watching. I forgot I was the guy that started just last Monday. It came to me that nobody left until I finished and the counts were balanced.

I said to Angelo, "I'm slow. I guess I'll get caught up on tearing and get through the tickets late this afternoon." I started tearing pulps one at time. Angelo said, "You grab a handful and break the back." He grabbed about twelve between his thumb and a couple of fingers and the stacks were headed for the sack.

"You guys stop what you're doing, get caught up here before lunch." What would have taken me two hours took just a few minutes. Lombard was just getting on the elevator. He rode up alone, leaving everybody else to walk upstairs to get to the guy with the cart selling hot dogs.

We were finished by three o'clock. With all the delays, nobody looked happy. I was last in the payroll line. I didn't open the envelope until I was on the streetcar. It was five two-dollar bills. Lombard had the last word but now – he owed me.

I called Peg to help me celebrate my first payday. She was glad I got a job. She was afraid I would start a booze delivery business again and she had forgotten to tell me about Repeal. There was a pause – then a quiet voice, "And Romans not here to save your butt!" I welcomed her quick change in mood. She had gotten a Ford convertible for her birthday and I hadn't seen it so let's just take a long ride.

It was quite a car, navy blue, the top was down and soft music played on the radio. I was not surprised we were parked on Art Hill and the sun had set. The radio played on, small talk, but I was in a trance. St. Louis U. – Was it the week just passed that I stumbled into Peg? I will think about fate tomorrow. I had five twos and was ready for all that was ahead. What is euphoria? I was just where I belonged. Music and the moon prevailed – healthy, seventeen and Art Hill after dark. Not wild adventure but togetherness, then to realize there was a spark that was new and to know the spark was shared. Peg broke the spell, "You deserve better, Bro – we both do, but it won't happen. Let's go home." We were half-way there. It was clear to us both the spell lived on.

We talked on the patio, I described the week from unloading vans to tearing pulp magazines. She was fascinated with the name "Sal" and my checking delivery trucks on Tuesdays. "Sal must have black curls and skinny hips" – a soft kiss. I peddled home the old familiar path – Euphoria riding on my shoulder.

Monday I was more tolerated than repelled. I was catching on to the routines and since I was doing something different, they left me alone. Angelo obviously had a different status than the rest of them. They were at a distance, maybe a bit afraid of him. Mr. Rogan, or "Lombard," was everywhere still saying nothing.

The sun came up on Tuesday but suddenly a cloudy sky. I was getting better at checking the magazines going in the trucks. Drivers were all surly, some thinking I could not count. They backed off, as the Lombard always just happened to pop up close by. All clouds parted, a navy blue convertible roared into the parking lot across the street horn blowing. A baseball cap and ponytail atop her head, wearing a sweater a bit too tight, Peg sat on top of the driver's seat waving a box in the air yelling, "Hey Bro! Take off early! I brought lunch and a bottle of wine."

I bounced across the street, grabbed the lunch and got her the hell out of the area before a riot could get started. She blew the horn again. As she drove off she yelled "Say Hi to Sal."

I walked back across the street as though nothing had happened. The hot dog guy was pushing up and the lunch line was forming. Lombard happened to be watching close by. I received a lot of side-glances and heard many remarks that I ignored. I thought it was all forgotten. I was in error.

Hope wrote regularly and so did I. I told her all about my job and she told me about all the parties at finishing school. Wondered why she never commented on my carrier adventures at the News Company.

I had not told either Hope or Peggy about the day that all the guys but Sal were having fun. One of the guys would clap his hands and all the others would yell, "Sal has 'em." I had avoided the small can; I did not want to get involved with any co-worker in close quarters. The sink for washing hands was outside the room. I had easy access to the rear of a truck in the parking lot across the street for regular use. To be on the safe side I called Doctor Mudd. He said, "You did right. Wash your hands regularly; do not pay any attention otherwise. There is only one way to get claps or pregnant. Toilet seats do not get involved. By all means don't date any girlfriends of your coworkers." I wondered if that Rhett Butler guy had ever worked with a guy with claps. I damn well knew he couldn't tear a stack of "Love Story" pulps.

For the first time I felt ready to talk to Jim and Virginia. Other than Roman, they were the only ones whose opinions mattered. St. Louis U. was a humbling memory, but now I had my pride restored. For what it was worth, I had a job.

Jim answered the phone, Virginia was out shopping but they had been expecting my call. Why had it taken me so long? I told him I had just gotten a job. He was not surprised. Virginia had a dinner well planned and they had been waiting, the entrée was to be on me. White Castle had been advertising a "Sack of Six," that was it. I was to bring it the following Saturday at six-thirty. Virginia had made the plan over a month ago and that was the way it was to be.

I wore my graduation suit, it was the first time I put it on since my job interview. I picked up the "Sack of Six" and a side order of pickles, the bill was thirty cents. I was seeing their apartment for the first time but I had long known what it would be like. Jim, too, had worn a suit and Virginia was as always the perfect picture.

Everything was just what I knew it had to be. Lighted candles were on the table. It was set for three. Not paper plates but bone china, crystal glasses and silver by every plate. It was filet mignon in that White Castle bag I carried and the pickles were Béarnaise sauce. There were cups of cold potato soup with green onions; Virginia said it was some French name, and white wine.

Jim had run water on the bag of White Castles and put it in the oven. After the soup, Virginia brought out the entrée on a fancy platter. The warm White Castle burgers were on the rim of the platter and a baseball scoop of crusty mashed potatoes was in the middle. A second dish with white asparagus and little carrots was in her other hand.

We had all been talking at the same time and each not hearing what the other said. They knew that Roman had wandered afar and that I had been seeing Peggy with Hope away again. Virginia was enthusiastic to hear of Peggy but it was clear that she liked Hope. I could not understand why she did not like somebody she had never seen but Virginia could do no wrong.

They thought Peggy bringing a picnic lunch to the News Company was hilarious. When I told them I went to the bathroom behind a truck, Virginia said if I were arrested, she would swear that my bad reputation was only half deserved.

Better friends no one ever had but all good times have to end. Jim insisted on driving me home. Virginia hugged me whispering, "Be sure to take care of yourself." Jim was serious on the drive home. He said I was probably too late to think about St. Louis U. for the January term but to plan on next September. He told me that not many men could rip a six-inch stack of pulps. I needed to be sure to learn everything there was to learn. The Lombard would not teach me anything, but remember I could learn a lot from him. I was to be surprised again; Jim, too, knew just where I lived. He stopped right at the front door. We just shook hands, nothing left to say.

It was again no time to sleep with so much to plan, but how to do it? I was parked on the porch rail just staring at the sky. My mother came out and stood beside me, just to share the vacant sky. Suddenly she squeezed my hand, and then she was inside the house again. I wished I had put my arm around her, but I was too late, by then she was gone.

Peg and I were suddenly a pair. A protective concern each for the other – thoughts were shared but feelings guarded. There was a relationship of deep trust and mutual pride but vacant dreams. Emotion was on hold for someone else; it was temporary from the outset. Both knew but did not admit; the torch burned bright – it was not for them. It was not only Peg that held it all together; I felt the same for her. We were saving each other from ourselves.

Finally, it was Thanksgiving and Hope was home. She would not be home for Christmas, and would start Vassar next September. Her parents were going east for the holidays. Hope would be taking her final semester in France; she was so happy with the plans. She would miss me and we would "Write often."

I had been giving my mother eight bucks a week: carfare, lunch, church, etc., left me with twelve bucks in my bank. I bought a string of pearls at the jewelry store on Grand Avenue – eight bucks on sale. They came in a black leather box; I remember a gold crest on the flap. It cost sixty cents to mail them insured for ten bucks. I left the post office feeling all alone, wondering if I had been left behind. Did I really care?

Suddenly it was the day before Christmas; the magazine business is normally dead during the holidays. Returns are heavy. Dealers want to clean out and get credits due in the current year.

A black Packard parked in front, a guy in a white fedora was followed by a pair of tough-looking goons. One was carrying a box of stick salamis and the other a box of bottles of Chianti. I knew the guy in the hat must own the office next to Mr. Rogan. He hugged Angelo, gave him an envelope, and a kiss on the cheek. The goons gave him a stick of salami and a bottle of Chianti. The same routine followed for the other men minus the hug. I got an envelope from a different pocket, along with the wine and salami but no hug or kiss. He gave me a friendly punch in the stomach and said, "You're good at numbers but 'Babes' ain't for the job." He left with "Merry Christmas and tomorrow get to church." The Lombard did not wish anything, he followed them out the door, and everybody knew that he belonged. I got a punch in the gut instead of the hug and kiss – I was not one of the "group."

Jim called to wish me Merry Christmas from them both. He had a promotion and now had to travel a bit. They were taking a Christmas cruise and hoped to have a baby soon. They would call later.

Peg was delighted to be labeled a "Babe" by an expert on babes. Her folks were celebrating their twenty-fifth wedding anniversary on New Year's Eve and we were expected at the party. It was formal, lucky it was after dark so my neighbors did not see my tuxedo. I walked to her house and we went to the country club in her car.

We were not the first to arrive; we had a large table right off the dance floor. The cocktails, wine and steaks were great. Waiters carried around drinks and trays of snacks. Champagne was served and song filled the darkened room. There was a toast at midnight. According to some tradition, the chef was serving five trays of herring in different wines and slivers of capon.

We were on the dance floor when Peg said, "My folks are staying here tonight. We will tell them we are leaving to go to church." It was a night none could ever forget! We had scrambled eggs, lox, and Champagne for breakfast. I had never heard of lox before and didn't know it was fish. Peg wanted to take a bike ride. I said I'd look stupid on a bicycle in a tux even in her neighborhood. She came back with a sweat suit, still wrapped in its original packing. "My dad has a stack of these," she said. There were four bikes in the garage. We rode about five miles to the park and back. We ended up on the patio not wanting this time to ever end – but knew it had to. "You won't want me to drive you home. Keep the sweats; he doesn't know how many of anything he has. I put your suit in a box. Bring the bike back anytime." We held hands; the looks exchanged had said it all. I peddled off that same path home.

Back to work. Attitudes were more aggressive: a lot of laughing about their bonus, five bucks each, they knew I got less, he took mine from a different pocket, and me bringing a broad to work. We were doing returns when things came to a head. I had been there about three months and didn't care that nobody talked to me. Now they were all talking about me, to my face, and that is what they intended.

It got to be more fun for "Fat Tony" as the week went by. He had always been the leader. Friday morning, I had learned to destroy the pulps without the glue tearing the skin between thumb and fingers. When you grabbed a stack do not stretch your fingers, leave the first joint slightly bent. The secret is to get a grip. You have to squeeze the stack; it will not break if it is loose. I was forming the opinion that I could break anything in half that I could hold.

I was taking out my frustrations on pulp magazines. I thought it was an accident when Tony knocked over the stack of magazines that I was attacking and I had to stack them up again. I knew damn well it was no accident when he knocked them on the floor the next time. I was picking them up when I heard them all laughing. I was raising up when the knife ring on his finger contacted my upper lip. I heard more than felt the knife blade scraping teeth. Anger consumes when your mouth is full of your own blood and you do not know if you are going to die. I recalled later that I growled, "You son of a bitch."

Now, and in ever-vivid memory, is the pent up rage – promise and denial, frustration, insult, and contempt – twelve bucks a week, a job that belonged to me. My fist contacted his backbone where his stomach was just in the way – he doubled over as my knee met his nose. I fell on top of him intending to dent the concrete floor with his head. His friends moved in as I heard, "Get your ass upstairs! Get a block of ice."

Lombard was picking me up, his hands under both arms, and we were on the elevator as if I was a small sack of potatoes. He had grabbed a pack of paper towels and shoved them in my hand. They soaked up a lot of blood around my mouth just as I threw up. Sal ran up to the elevator as we hit the main floor with ice in a towel (I didn't care where he got it). Lombard put the ice up to my mouth. The ice and towel slowed the bleeding. He gave me a jacket with the News Company name on the back like the truck drivers wore, and we went out the back door. He handed me my pay envelope saying, "Stay home tomorrow but Monday be back at work. Call your doctor as soon as you get home." He told a truck driver to take me home.

The driver was not happy but Lombard had spoken more words in the last fifteen minutes than I had heard in the last three months. I told the driver to go out Delmar to Skinker then turn right. I ignored his remarks and his gaze. I told him to go left when we got to Olive Street Road and I'd tell him when to stop. I didn't want him to be able to find me some dark night. Anger was returning. I felt I had been set up, but why? The five guys may have had an idea, but Angelo and Lombard must have been close by. I told the driver to "go out Olive Street Road to Route 66, then you'll be in my neighborhood – better get your ass back home. Tell them all I'll be there Monday."

Luckily it was Friday and nobody was home. I called Dr. Mudd. The nurse said he was busy with another patient and would call back. He did about an hour later, and said that Mr. Lombard had called and had told him what had happened. Even though I had stopped bleeding, I should still come to the hospital right away. Streetcar conductors and their passengers view you with reserve when your mouth is the size of a baseball and you are trying to cover it with a wet towel. The hospital front desk hustled me into the emergency ward; my looks did not fit the lobby image.

I had to wait awhile before a nurse took me to a curtained alcove. Dr. Mudd came in saying, "You were lucky to be cut in the mouth. It is easier to fix than a nose. Get rid of that damn towel!" The nurse took it and threw it in a covered can. He never stopped talking. He had said he wanted to see the knife that had cut me and they had a truck bring it out. (I did not tell him I had my ring knife in my pocket). He was swabbing my mouth with a stick that I could not see. He was talking to the nurse. "Lucky this blade is razor sharp and has a narrow point. His finger made it drag, that is why his lip is gashed but it's deep only in the puncture area and the point penetrated to pierce the upper gum. It may bother a tooth later but nothing to do now. The puncture is clean and bled well, all soft tissue on the inside and it is beginning to adhere now. Don't close the surface, it could become infected. The resident will do the stitching; he is thinking of going into plastics so he needs the practice."

He finally recognized me. "You will be OK in a few days; things in the mouth heal quickly. Infection is the only problem. If it looks bad in the next five days, call me." The resident was delighted to stitch my lip saying I would not have any scars as he put in eight tight stitches, but there was no way to close the penetration point. I would have a scar there but it would fade. Come back Wednesday to get the stitches out. I left with a strip bandage across my upper lip all the way across my face. The cashier said that the News Company paid the bill.

My mother was shocked. I told her that the elevator gate slipped and hit me in the mouth. It was all right, but the company doctor wanted me to look good. Peggy called, a friend was having a birthday, she needed a date, and I was the only one in town. She thought it was funny that I had a split lip. I would be a hero that just escaped from the dessert. Instead, she announced to the party that I did not have a disease, that I was just getting used to heavy kissing.

Monday I got to work early. I had a job and twelve bucks a week and nobody was going to screw it up. I was surprised when everybody tried to stay out of my way, no hostile scowls. I was glad to see that Tony had a heavy tape across his nose and two black eyes.

About ten o'clock the big boss appeared. He rode up on

the elevator with the guys who had finished unloading the vans. He got right to the point. "Something happened last Friday that should not have happened and won't happen again." He pointed to me, "The company is moving you upstairs on Fridays and Saturdays to check the counts." He punched me on the arm.

"Ya proved ya got balls, come on up front, I'll show you what to do." The Lombard just watched, he followed the big boss and I fell in behind. We went into his office. They sat down, him behind the desk, I still stood.

"The Company likes the way you have taken to the business. We want to send you to learn bookkeeping. First at Browns Business, they know you are coming by – they will be there until six so you have time to get there after work. Here is their card." I took the card and left. I was choked up, I had not expected it.

Peggy was elated I was promoted and going to business school. She was making it just routine but I knew she was proud of me. I got carried away and told her the boss had said, "Ya proved ya got balls." She said she wanted to meet the boss. She punched me on the arm, "Ya proved ya got balls."

Brown Business School was not St. Louis U. but it was a way back. I had been booked for the entrance program with a semester in bookkeeping that started in March. I would have the follow-up program and a certificate awarded in "Business Administration." Accounting Fundamentals, Tax Law, and Audit, classes were to follow. It was a two-year program. I will see them in March. I was about to become indebted but fate intervened. A lady from Mr. Hannigan's office had called. I should contact Mr. Butler, he had an interview for me.

The interview was with Standard Oil (Indiana). A New Deal sponsored Work/College Program. I smelled success. My shortened student life had exhibited my acceptance at St. Louis University School of Commerce. I had all textbooks and already some campus familiarity – I was on my way. I got the job – now a product of The New Deal. They wanted me to start on the fifteenth of the month to match their pay periods. I had six free days!

I went first to the News Company. It had not been all fun but it was my first job and they had been the first to pay me every week. It was the first time Mr. Rogan saw me in a suit but he did not seem to notice. I told him I was thankful for them hiring me but I had a better opportunity and I was giving a week's notice. He did not say a word, but picked up the phone. I didn't try to hear what he said. He then told me it was better that I leave now as they only wanted people that were in the family; I could pick up my pay at the cash window. He walked out. I wanted to shake hands, I owed him and he had taught me more than either of us realized. I lingered a moment; I wrote "Thanks" on the back of two of my cards. I left one in "Lombard's" office and one for the big boss. I picked up my last eight bucks at the cash window – then I was away.

My next stop was St. Louis U. I was welcomed into the night program. The semester had started a week before but I had textbooks and class assignments, there were vacancies, so the only problem would be my catching up with the two classes I had missed. I started school that night. My classmates were all much older than I was but no one seemed to pay any attention to anything but class.

I slept late the next day, Friday; it was the first free day, other than Sundays, in many months and with all the things going on I had been out of contact with the outside world. There was a note from yesterday; Peggy was having a party Saturday night. I called but she was out, I left word with the maid that I would be there. Then I found another message; Hope had called on Wednesday. I wondered why she had not written. I called; she was just walking out the door. Could I come over or was I at work? She would be back at five, it was now just past twelve. I thought I would like to surprise her in my grey flannel suit and tell her about my new career at Standard Oil.

I was surprised when her mother opened the door and even more surprised when she hugged me. No kiss, just a hug, and a feeling cheek to cheek as she said, "So glad to see you!" We had talked by phone just after New Years, just two weeks ago. Her father was too jovial, slapping me on the back, he had just heard that I had an interview at Standard Oil and wished me all good luck. He had ushered me to the bar and his wife disappeared.

He took a fancy bottle and a pair of short glasses from a shelf. "This is Haig Pinch, my favorite scotch blend. All single malts have a flavor and to me it takes a blend." I knew he was talking because he did not know what to say. He had poured a measure of Scotch and a squirt of water in the glasses telling me about no ice.

Hope appeared in the doorway; again, a wispy vision. Her father picked up one glass and went out the door behind her. No anxious hugs, no hungry kiss. She came across the room. "We have to talk." I got there first, giving her a fatherly kiss on her forehead. "Yes, your father said you knew about the interview with Standard Oil. Well I took the job and took the plunge. I will be carrying a full sixteen hours at St. Louis U. I sold my soul to the company store for the rest of the time."

Hope had taken the other glass I had not touched; she was pouring the liquid into the sink. There was no better way to say, "Good-bye."

I had a report due for my Economic History class Monday night, I explained. I noticed she was wearing the Christmas pearls, I wondered, why?

The Saturday party was strained at first. Hope was there with a guy in a Yale blue jacket, she obviously did not expect to see me there. Peggy took over and everyone relaxed as she introduced Hope's friend. She said he was in town to collect money for a New Progressivism, she did not know what that was, but she thought "James the Third" was cute and nobody had any money anyhow.

Later in the evening, Peggy and I happened to be alone and I told her I knew she set Hope up – she did not expect to see me here. She said, "Sure and how does a cold fish look next to a big boss? Certified 'Babe' like me?" I was confused but I knew I had been the one she cared about.

The next day, Sunday, I rode the bicycle from New Years back to Peg. It was right we met on the patio. Before I could say a word, she said, "I heard about 'you and the company store.' My parents have told me I have to settle down. Dad wants me to go to Rutgers, but Mom votes for Swarthmore. I told them anywhere but Vassar."

We both had earned a quiet pause. I said, "It was not all it should have been – it should have been another, a different time."

"Yes, but that's the way it was – I can't forget the one who never said 'I love you.' He was the one – I always wished that would have said it." Now it was she who punched my arm. "You will make it big, Bro – 'Ya proved ya got balls'."

She walked away, she did not look back. It was right; we never met again. It was the same route home – this time I walked, maybe too slow. I would not pass this way again.

Virginia called, they had heard about Standard Oil and that I was entered at St. Louis U. They knew I was up to my ears, call them when I could.

CHAPTER SEVEN

THE COMPANY WAY

Standard Oil was not a company, it was an institution. The last time somebody was hired, he was somehow related to somebody. He was hired because somebody else had died. Guys who had spent their working lives there didn't like strangers. Someone ten years younger who was getting more attention was resented. I had no friend but did not care; I had bought the store. It was not my first time out. I had learned the rules. I had a brand new heart; it bled Red Crown Gasoline.

Hardship was not everywhere. There was a world apart where people laughed and played, where worry did not take the place of sleep. Attitude and commitment to God and country stayed the same, but conscience waffles with the whims of style. I was in a cloistered, guarded world; admittance was only by decree.

Two ten-year-old altar boys broke the code; they put me on the way – a faster track, no looking back. Ambitions are the same at any age, only time and circumstance change. Fate defines a happening – Life only defines that you were born. Destiny is not within the stars, it is within us.

Two years of long hours, study, and sweat but it was combined with the sweet smell of success. I had become a token in the corporate structure. To the headquarters in Chicago, and the Regional Manager in St. Louis. I was the "Performing Monkey" in a joint experiment. The government had engaged headquarters in an exercise in upward mobility. Every conniving corporate prince fought to be associated with the success or the first to damn the failure of anything of interest in his "Upstairs Mobility." I was held at a distance waiting for my back to be exposed. I accidentally overheard a remark, "Yeah, and we may be reporting to the bastard someday." I will remember what you called me – you alleged component of a man.

It was a Friday, all events at Standard Oil seemed to relate with Friday and a pay period. I was called to Mr. Jantzen's office. He had remained my point of contact as I had been regularly shifted to various departments. Mr. May, the Regional Manager, was seated at Mr. Jantzen's desk, occupying a side chair. It seemed natural that it be a Friday and for Jantzen to speak while Mr. May observed; this was the Standard Oil way. Mr. May and headquarters had decided that I switch now to law school. I had met the minimum entrance criteria of sixty credit hours and other endorsements and I had been accepted at Benton Law School. "Headquarters will assume all costs and you will be under their review in addition to the personal observation of Mr. May. Benton Law will be submitting regular reviews and you are to submit your experiences monthly in writing to Mr. May."

Mr. May now got up and departed without saying a word. Mr. Jantzen occupied his chair; he too seemed to have nothing more to say and was busy now with the papers on his desk. I was in shock; I had been ordered and dismissed, "Salute and Carry On." I backed out the door, but I was walking ten feet off the ground.

I returned to my desk and buried my head in papers that I could not see. I think I spent much time in humble prayer. I had just been relieved of all college costs. This economic drain had caused some strain but more importantly, they had chosen me without thought for me. Benton Law School had first accepted Standard Oil, then incidentally, me. The school was the product of the St. Louis legal body being uncomfortable with the lowering constitutional curricula of law schools in general, so they had embarked on their own. They accepted fewer than ten students in a semester and not all survived.

Dedicated but also successful local attorneys taught the

three-year accredited program. Most students were employed in the legal field; late evening and weekend classes were standard. It was a choice that I would have traded much to achieve but the choice had been made for me. I had already heard that I was scheduled for Northwestern Graduate Business School. Someday, would there be a choice made for me at a price too high for me to pay?

I had run across Hope's class ring. I had discarded it in a rarely used drawer. I had intended to donate it to a scholarship fund. I do not know why, but it came to me now as an achievement award.

I had long coveted a handsome leather briefcase in the window of my favorite jewelry store on Grand Avenue. The jeweler was delighted. The briefcase was ten bucks and he could give me twenty for the ring. He remarked that it must be from a rich school for class rings to be made 14 carat. I stopped at 905 Liquors, I owed myself a nickel beer, more to think than drink.

All memories are meant to fade,
Hope a love of innocence;
Peggy, a love of meaning.

What is there to go back to? To do again? I wonder what Hope did with my high school diploma? Do commitments die if made by one alone?

I went across Grand Avenue and dropped the extra ten bucks in the St. Anthony Poor Box at the College Church.

The final chapter
– ten bucks for ambition
– ten bucks for the good of others
– let St. Anthony decide.

CHAPTER EIGHT

LIFE GOES ON

The second term of FDR was the time of deepest hardship; the New Deal had failed its promise. It was now viewed by many as the cause of extended pain. Fading hope was all there was but hope still served. The charm of FDR had captured the nation's soul.

It was the increasing demands of the war in Europe that brought suffering to an end. The industrial might of the nation was rekindled, men found work, tragedies were in the past, not forgotten, but now were memories etched in a remote and distant time.

The War brought horror before unknown but, for the moment, only the release from tragedy was felt; the world would never be the same.

Did it have to be on Friday once again? Mr. Jantzen called, this time he was alone but the scene was the same, the tone unchanged. He was abrupt. The entire petroleum industry was now under government control; all products would be distributed as allocated. Sales activities were to cease, division offices closed. All employees were being advised to provide for themselves; only a few would be retained. My account at Benton was covered for the current semester but any future charges would be mine. Standard Oil would furnish any personal recommendation as merited. All would be promptly advised as changes occurred; two months separation pay, a ten-day notice applied.

A "ten-day notice." It was the Chicago Office's way, but what else to expect? I had crashed the corporate ladder but it was not, now, the only life I knew. It was not the shock to me that it must be to guys who worked there all their lives but more attention had come to me. I had seized all opportunities but doors had been opened to me that to others had been closed. I owed much to FDR. He was to be condemned by many but it was the New Deal Program that had opened the doors for me. He is remembered by me and many others in times of prayer.

A new airplane company had approached me at law school; they wanted me to come out for an interview. I called for an appointment and was introduced to a new and different life. I was directed to an alcove where a young lady gave me a four-page form and watched while I filled it out. I had to list: all the schools I had attended, where I had lived throughout my life, all relatives including cousins and grand-parents. It also asked if I had ever been arrested or in jail. Some fifteen minutes later I had completed the form, she put it in an envelope, which she carefully sealed. Then she advised me that I had completed a Government Security request – that was the first requirement since the Company was engaged in classified work. She took the envelope to an office across the hall.

She advised me that their representative who had contacted me at Benton Law School had submitted a favorable report. I was scheduled for testing that would consume the remainder of the morning. My test results would be reviewed and employment interviews were scheduled for the next morning. I was to go to the security station at the main entrance and a security guard would escort me from there.

The next day was impressive. Security guards did not look like policemen, their uniform was a military-looking cap with a big holstered gun clearly visible on their hip. The main guard asked my name. I was sure that he took me to be a foreign spy and if I forgot my name a big gun would be in my face and I would see a guard who would want to shoot me.

He motioned for me to stand against the wall; I was busy trying to get my feet inside the footprints on the floor when another guy behind a camera I was in front of snapped a picture. The first guy grabbed my wrist and pulled me over to the table next to the camera. He then proceeded to stick my fingers on an ink pad and then onto a card. The camera guy had taken the camera into a closet and came out with my picture on a card that was attached to a cord. He shoved it over my head, then gave the negative to the first guy who put it with my fingerprints into an envelope. He sealed the envelope and both guards initialed the envelope and put it through a slot on the top of the table.

He waved a lady over who wore the same type of cap but had no gun. The two guys gave me cold stares and silence as she said, "Come with me." We walked to another building; I remarked about the weather, she scribbled on a note pad strapped on her belt as she ignored my comment about the weather. We entered a lobby where an attractive young lady sat at a desk. Some twenty people were waiting on chairs around two of the walls. The guard led me to a door, then suddenly turned around facing me with her back to the door; she was trading hand signals with the desk clerk.

The lady at the desk picked up a phone; in a few seconds a buzzer sounded, the door was opened from the inside and the guard stepped aside. Another young lady said, "Welcome to personnel." For the last half hour, I had been photographed, finger printed, and under suspicion – I had heard but five words; "name," "stand here" and "follow me." Why should I say, "thanks" or "good-bye" to my stoic escort? I stepped inside, and the door abruptly closed behind me.

Mrs. Ritter, Employment Manager, was polite but cold. My test results were favorable and an offer of employment was to be made but she first wanted me to be aware of company policies. More than one division had interest in me but overall company interests were her only concern. There was a shortage of engineering talents and first attention was directed to this priority.

The existing technical resources of the company were deployed to promote the accelerated education of certain selected employees to fill vacancies. Classes after working hours were conducted by former professors who were now in industry as a patriotic choice. Class sizes were very small, affording the advantages of individual attention. Credit-hour recognition would accrue toward a Certificate of Award by Washington University after completion of a six-week Trainee Exercise of employment in Production and other essential departments of operation. Trainee interest and commitment demonstrated in the fifty-cents per-hour wage, a written weekly report to be submitted each Monday morning, uncompensated extra hours expected, twenty dollars the maximum weekly stipend.

I was given a ten-page handbook of details. She hoped I would become an Engineering Trainee but the choice was mine. "Please review the handbook and come directly to this building at seven-thirty tomorrow morning, register at the desk; they will ask if you are a "trainee." Depending on your choice you will be picked up for a final interview. You have joined the Team." She wished me every success. I knew this is where I now belonged.

I went back to Standard Oil for the final time. I informed Mr. Jantzen that I was employed by the Airplane Company we shook hands. He told me I had impressed a lot of people. I had been on a rocket to the top; it was too bad it had to end. He would process my final papers as ending the fifteenth (it was the company way).

I would get two months pay and I had some credit in the Stock Plan that normally were awarded after ten years but I would get cash now because of the closing. My final check would be mailed on the fifteenth. He told the secretary to make up the papers for me to sign; he went into his office, the door closed. We never met again.

I remembered my packet of calling cards. As the secretary typed the papers I wrote, "Thanks" on the back of one and asked her to give it to him. She looked at my card, then suddenly kissed me on the cheek and told me that everybody liked me. I knew she exaggerated but I was glad she did. I mumbled good-bye. I patted her on the shoulder, there was no one else to see, I had no words to leave behind.

I walked to the corner – I realized I had stopped and turned around – I took a long look back, then walked up Olive Street as I had done so many times on my way to St. Louis U. There were memories I took with me, happenings that were only mine. I walked about two blocks, there was a street car coming and I got on. Soon I was walking on an old familiar street. All Saints Church was a block away.

The church was locked, I sat on the steps, the Angelus bell was ringing – I had turned my life around, and it had just struck noon – now I had to think.

The Standard Oil check would be mailed next Wednesday, two months extra pay – the fifteenth and a Friday, my final touch, it was the company way. I had no problem with six weeks at twenty dollars each. There were now new rules, new faces nothing quite the same. I knew that the trainee program was for me. Fifty-cents per-hour was the price of entry; there were other tests ahead, nothing to be free. Fingerprints, guards with guns, Standard Oil was in that other world that was no more.

It had not been concern for the future but a return to where I first found value – myself. Where once before my world was changed and the fates had intervened. Zito and the Assistant Pastor and how three ten-year-old altar boys were joined in spirit, a bond to long endure. Here was the American Legion baseball and that social life – suits in navy blue, grey flannel, and a tailored tuxedo. Ten years – different challenges, each had heard a different drum, each had followed the path that called. Wide separation, the bonding to be ever strong but the intimacy was gone.

A police car had driven by a couple of times but now a cop got out and told me the church was open only on Sundays, never at night. He suggested that it was not a good idea for me to be sitting here and it was not safe here after dark. I took his advice when he told me the street cars stopped running after six o'clock but there would be one going east in about ten minutes. I thanked him; I had an early class at Benton, I was on my way.

The Great Depression was the life I had come to really know. All Saints Church is where the script began – the doors now locked no service after dark. There is no better way to bracket the ten years that were enfolded. It was right that sundown be the final scene and Benton law school the closing chapter of that only phase of life I ever really knew.

There was no final class, Benton College of Law was closing, the faculty had all been called to a higher duty, the new national challenge had overcome the purpose of the college. All third-year students were being tutored for the bar examination, all expected to succeed. The records of all were being transferred to the City College of Law and Finance. A commercial enterprise was recently awarded consulting contracts under federal programs. The faculty wished everyone success, your worth had been proven, recommendations were offered and the facilities would be open and available for the next month. Mr. Copeland, the Director of Benton, gave us the word. He was a colonel in the Army Reserve and was being called to active duty at the end of the month. He would retire from the military and the legal practice after the war but would welcome any contact at any time.

I left the building, the final page was written, a new phase begun. Airplanes and a rising sun still a day away. Transition is for tomorrow, retrospect belonged to the remainder of that day. I had passed all tests, I had paid the price, everything I had I earned, but success was tied to where I was, what I wore and who met me there. I had been used by others but I had used them too in turn. Events don't just happen, they are ordained by some will on high. The six o'clock mass in a parish church, the scene of values professed and justice proclaimed in contrast with the intrigues of who served the six o'clock. The character of three ten-year-olds in the open contest of authority abused. It was this bonding in a common cause that brought me to the world that I knew then and will remain that blind commitment 'til the day I die.

Roman and Marty
Where to go?
Can two such Altar Boys
Be found again ?

CHAPTER NINE

TOMORROW TOO WILL KNOW A YESTERDAY

Where we are is always the product of that many yesterdays that compose the reality of now. Reflecting only on a near yesterday would ignore the context of the right and the wrong of how we got here, who did what to whom and why. Time passes as events transpire but faith and trust are characteristics that are inbred, the bedrock of commitment.

The Ten Commandments first defined the mandates of Creation as obligated; First to God and thence to man. Man relates to his fellow man in equal turn. Time immemorial depicts the defeat of conscience, the, void of precept that has prevailed in the centuries of, so-called, enlightened rule.

Sages from Socrates to Carl Marks, and countless theologies between, have theorized a state of being that is in contrast, often conflict, with the constancy professed. The inability of men to fairly govern another man has been the humbling challenge of maturing civilizations throughout the ages.

The ambitions of those who lust to rule absorb the dissemination of rights as the State sees fit. This fundamental is the axiom of Royal Rule. Abuse under such suppression leads to rightful revolt.

This nation was not conceived in compromise but in the positive of a declaration, the absolute of commitment, the solid core of individuals in pledge to each other and that all men are equal within that union of " "We the People"." This culture, this integrity of governing at the consent of the governed, is unique in the history of rule. These inherent qualities and a formal process for amending render the Constitution of the United States the envy of the world. The term "exceptional" applies.

Progressivism a failing ideology through stealth and deceit has penetrated critical function of performance. A brittle shell, an elite cult of collective rights and central rule has exploited an apathetic electorate. The Constitution is under siege.

The American Dream is a parable – the equal of all other men with unalienable rights endowed by their creator is real. "We the People": government under consent of we the governed is reality. No other government in the history of human rule has been so construed.

The laws of Nature prompt that all need properly to aid all other men, but self-responsibility is the individual demand of equality as orderly conduct is a demand of freedom.

Search for a fellow man that you might ask if first he has served himself. Respect then how he in turn maybe of aid to you. He is of "We the People" and so are You.

CHAPTER TEN

WHAT HAPPENS NEXT?

Nineteen hundred and thirty is a year inscribed in the annuls of hardship and despair. The Great Depression now seems unreal but the scars of tragedy will long endure. World War I had ended some twelve years before – it was World War II that saw it end. The story of my life was within the bookends of two wars. (Can any war or any depression be rightly called "Great?")

The wars did not start here nor did this nation intervene by popular choice. The constant conflicts in Europe were rooted in economic decline. Contrasting forms of Socialism were governing throughout the continent. This duplicity was contrary to the German dreams of a "One World Order." The first ambition of the Prussian Aristocracy was a United States of Europe under German domination. Bismarck, economist philosopher and advocate of wealth spread, was the anointed leader. Bismarck was an expert in planning, organization and structured discipline. His carefully rehearsed presentations of a top down form of governing and centralized control attracted the entrenched bureaucracies in the capitals of Europe.

The history of all European nations is portrayed in an ever-repeating sequence of war and peace, progress and decay. Each has known the joy of victory and the agony of defeat as controlled by the whim of royal rule. Abuse, the price of question, cruel group persecution of any organized dissent. The strong and venturing emigrated in search of freedom – oppression left behind. The British Empire extended beyond the setting sun. All lands ruled by King George through a parliament of the ruled. All lands equal but equal justice was denied. America the new land to the west was taxed too high and poorly represented. It was to here that emigrants had fled – from this base, America was born.

Thirteen Colonies found equal cause and strength in unity. They soon divorced the rule of king. The United States of America, a new and unique government – "all men are created equal, Life, Liberty and Property individually endowed by their Creator."

Another revolution had been fought in France – "Equality, Liberty, Brotherhood" granted by the state. The brutal conduct of the French Revolution did much to further divide an already divided Europe.

The precepts of the revolt in America were later defined in a Constitution of meaning. The strength in unity and thrust of purpose was defined. A vibrant national will was soon portrayed in deed and action. Thomas Jefferson, the third president of the new nation, boldly dispatched the United States Marines to the far distant Barbary Coast to enforce the nation's rights on the high seas. The Monroe Doctrine boldly proclaimed the protective concerns of the United States throughout the Western Hemisphere.

History unfolded as years passed. The War Between the States had purified the nation's soul but post-war adjustments failed. "Go West Young Man" was the challenge as the nation expanded in both territory and population. Victory in a short-lived war with Spain and the miracle of the Panama Canal infused the nation once again.

The conquests of Napoleon were the ultimate product of the bloody French Revolt. Socialism was welding all of Europe into one common economic hope with local political appeal. It was Jacques Laval' in Paris, the Socialists in Belgium, and the Social Democrats in Germany, the best of Europe, all searching for autonomy within that common cause: of Economic Hope. German aggression in Central Europe – adventures from

Russia south to the Mediterranean was of increasing concern to England, Russia and the lesser powers of Europe. The fundamentals of Bismarck's Philosophy were the foundation of the German thrust and relative appeal.

This contra-culture was of growing interest in the elitists' academia circles in the United States. Bismarck the anointed leader, an icon, but John Hopkins University was the seat of power. Richard Ely, Bismarck disciple, was the soul. Ely, an advocate of the Hagel Theory of apportioned wealth, was not dedicated to planning or organization. He was the phantom soon-forgotten spirit. Men who never heard of him are moving to the measure of his thoughts – now dead over one hundred years. He wrote dozens of books on taxes, land use, urban reform and several texts on general economics. A leader of the new generation of German-trained PhDs. In 1881, he began teaching at the newly formed John Hopkins University (conceived as a German style institution). Less than a decade later, his writings were considered to be of wider and more positive influence on American Legislation than the works of any other economist of the time. As a professor at John Hopkins and later at the University of Wisconsin, he was known as the Dean of American Economics. He mentored the major progressive thinkers and activists. The most famous members of Ely's gallery were politicians: Teddy Roosevelt, Woodrow Wilson and Robert La Follett Sr. Ely rejected non-Christian socialism, Marxist faith in abstract Universal Laws, atheism and anarchy. He favored a Golden Mean whereby a paternalistic state intervened under the instructions of experts to promote the true socialism of the kingdom of heaven.

Herbert Crowley, who became known as the "American" Bismarck, was born in 1869. His early education was in Paris and he continued to be addicted to French political philosophy. He considered his culture to be mainly French. His aim was to found the Republic on a Francophile footing. He left Harvard before graduating; his book "Promise of American Life" sold poorly but propelled him to the national stage where he drew the interest of Teddy Roosevelt who was the first to call him the "American" Bismarck. Crowley showed nothing but contempt for English liberalism; he preferred as he termed it, the efficiency and the greater equity of Germany. These tenants were fundamental in his theory of Liberalism. Liberals reluctantly accepted his insistence that America follow the German path that only higher education could create the professional leadership needed to run Society.

Oliver Wendell Holmes set forth the essence of Progressivism as a legal theory. He was a practitioner so his judgments reflect a coherent account of Progressivism in a distinctly legal as opposed to a philosophical or a practical instrument, though it is certainly all three. The legal aspect is of importance since it is the judicial branch of government that would pursue progressive theology most comprehensively. The appointment of Holmes to the Supreme Court was the first official act of Teddy Roosevelt as President.

John Dewey, through his volume of published articles and open activism, was a well-known figure. His many students had traveled far and wide and his popularity was widely spread. He was awarded a doctorate at John Hopkins University in 1864 where Richard Ely reigned. He held appointments in philosophy and education at both Chicago Universities and Columbia Universities. His distinguished career spanned fifty years. He played a significant role in the founding of the ACLU, the NAACP and the American Federation of Teachers. He was a regular contributor to Herbert Crowley's New Republic, the flagship journal of the Progressives. Dewey's social theory continues to be of political consequence. His conjecture of rights conferred by social order is a prerogative of state hypothesis.

Woodrow Wilson turned in direction of Crowley who no longer worshiped at the throne of Roosevelt. Wilson, who Crowley once reviled, was now his hero. Crowley was of significant influence in the Presidential election of 1912.

European conflict produced no victory, only the acceptance of the dominant force of the United States in world affairs. The nation was no longer considered a land of refugees, strangely governed and torn by civil war. Progress was related to economic wealth, physical energy, expanded territory, the shelter of distance and the protection of two oceans. This nation is uniquely – not strangely – governed and we were so divided from the peoples of Europe.

Decay is the fading pride and awareness of "We the People" consent of the governed individual control in contrast with an elitist cult addicted to contrary ideology.

Retrospectively, the temper of the times was best reflected in a speech nominating Teddy Roosevelt as the party candidate for president in the Progressive Party convention, 1903. "This new party has become the American exponent of a worldwide movement for social conditions. A movement which the United States, lagging behind other nations, has been unaccountably slow to become imbued in political action"

Nineteen hundred and thirty-six was the recognized low point of the so called Great Depression. Should this be the focal point of political transition, what attitudes were then distinct and why? Know first, that the then unemployed were mainly Veterans of World War One. Now in their mid-thirties, they had been denied their peak potential, their term of highest income and the satisfaction of success. Their vibrant youth, the dynamics of the economic structure of the nation, had been sacrificed to political deceit.

Woodrow Wilson, then president, was an avowed disciple of the social politics of Europe. Inaugurated under a Pledge of Trust, the oath he swore but ideals prevailed, his tour of harm was limited but the harm lived on.

The wars did not start here nor did this nation intervene by popular chance. Politics throughout Europe were rooted in dissent. Germany led the way, Bismarck, a brilliant economic philosopher as viewed by many but a radical by most. He was of diplomatic interest but ideological attractions prompted a rare personal involvement of the president of the United States both in entry in the conflict and the negotiation of the treaty of peace that followed.

The course of history and the maturing of this nation is portrayed in a sequence of progress and decay. All of Europe suffered the penalties of conflict; there was no victory, only the acceptance of the dominant force of the United States in world affairs. The nation was no longer considered a land of refugees strangely governed and torn by civil war. Progress was related to economic wealth, physical energy, expanded territory and the shelter of distance and the protection of two oceans. This nation is uniquely not strangely governed and we were so divided from the peoples of Europe. Decay is the fading pride and awareness of "We the People", consent of the governed individual control in contrast with an elitist cult addicted to contrary ideology.

The rescue of France and making the world safe for democracy was for many their first full night away from home. Once aware of the comforts in the city, return to a harsh farm life lost appeal; disrespect of authority, a decline in values and an ever-expanding urban culture was the end result. These changes were not experienced void of prior happening, a bitter civil war and adventures in conquest that were conceived in war with Spain.

Veterans of the First World War were neither victims nor survivors; they were alive to mourn the many they had to leave behind and to know the aftermath of change. It was my good fortune to know one well.

Ten-year-olds don't measure what they sense, they just walk away when they think there is something wrong. Character and conscience is inbred – ten-year-olds stay only where it's sound. Games and curiosity attract and there their world exists until high school comes along to end the fun and spoil the dreams. The triumvirate: Roman, Marty and I found a new association. A baseball field sponsored by the American Legion, the Stockholm Post 16, our team was the life anew.

Their rules were strict, you were a member of a team. Nobody cared where you lived or where you went to church or school. Everybody that played ball also cut the grass, but best of all you knew your coach was more than just a friend. The team won the title, we were all honorary members of Post 16 and we had a card to show it.

Reverting to declining rights – the politics of the times.

World War I had consumed the Wilson terms. American industrial might and military capacity had brought the triumph, it was so acknowledged throughout the world. A proud nation mourned the fallen as they honored all who wore the uniform of any branch of service. A humbled people grieved the somber truth of distant graves and the pain of the damaged hero who faced and feared an empty future – lonely and alone.

The widow, the Gold Star Mother, the orphan, their lives now vacant, support deprived, were joined in fervent prayer by a remembering few, but a fickle government soon forgot. The horrors of war, not just another thought left behind but a haunting cloud that someday would return.

The American spirit, awakened in a new and unfamiliar world – the economy flourished as life returned, "Hey, Prosperity Screw the War." There was "Prohibition" but there too was rejection of a stupid law. Bootleg booze, home brew and bathtub gin, and loud good times available any night at a friendly Speakeasy not far away.

The newly organized American Legion had purchased the long vacant Ritz Building, a neighborhood saloon, a victim of Prohibition. An impressive tower topped with a large American Flag and a new wing was added. The headquarters of an American Army Air Field, anywhere in France, had been duplicated. Post 16 Private Club – "Members Only" – was emblazoned on a brass plaque above the single entrance. A black wrought-iron gate fronted, the brass complimented, a dark-stained paneled door. The lobby freshly painted and newly carpeted. The marine grey walls were decorated with framed pictures: navy ships, an army tank and a bi-wing airplane. The only opening was a framed door, without knobs in the middle of the back wall that featured a matching framed panel that opened from the other side. A well-tailored lady of middle age occupied a polished desk to the side of the rear door; a large book, was on the top of the desk. A favorable impression, as intended, was conveyed. She would press a buzzer for an identified member who would then face visual review through the panel. The door would click open – you had been admitted.

The interior of the building had suffered most from lack of attention but was basically intact. The veterans had been exposed to the ambiance of British pubs and French wineries and had learned to appreciate the subtlety of atmosphere and the well appointed. Their talented labor was free, replacement materials were available from original source or salvaged from other abandoned saloons. Most significant was the pride and enthusiasm for which there was no price. The building was two stories, classical eight-foot ceilings of expanded sheet tin, which had been carefully restored. The reflective gold-flaked white walls dominated, the imposing atmosphere that had been hoped for was achieved. The upper floor, a now-favored big-party location, claimed a high rental. The main floor was divided down the middle, "Men Only" proclaimed on a brass plate above the narrow entrance to the right. A mahogany bar was visible across the back wall, as were polished dark wood tables and barrel chairs. The left side dominated as intended; a crystal chandelier had been donated from a river-front mansion being converted to apartments.

The right side was flagrantly declaring the planned privacy of past association; either higher relationship of wife or others was honored in the demonstration of respect and compliment dedicated to this commitment in the ambiance achieved, by the more spacious left side.

There was a deep psychology involved in the wall of division, or more correctly wall of unwanted separation. They had been forced to live another life, one burned into a mental compartment of regret, but no way to forget the horrors that life had brought. There was solace only in the camaraderie of those who shared. Military manuals snub civilians, a cult of junior officers, yet to know the academy ring twisters, blabbed that they were somehow ordained and are apart. The sight of blood, the stench of death they were yet to know, would purify their mind. Frankly, there was not one veteran who gave a damn.

Any appraisal in the raw terms of the time would first address the naked fact. It was circumstances that controlled happenings not anticipated, no escape. Men of different background, education, religion, environment and anything else were suddenly mingled in a cause and purpose they would not have elected to defend. They had been trained not to think but to react on instinct that was contrary to their upbringing. Suddenly they were in a foreign land, new language, open morals. Too soon the battlefront – life in a muddy trench, always rain and the smell of decay. Food out of a can you opened with your bayonet – no thought of what you stuck before, rotten food was not the problem; the damn stuff was greasy cold. Two hours sentry duty every four hours. Shoot by instinct if you heard a fart or just thought something moved – Shoot, Don't think! The curses and the bullets were intended to condemn – the thing that moved would never move or ever fart again. The only reason for living was to keep your buddy next to you alive and to know that you were his buddy and he thought the same. There was that constant fog close to the ground it was always hard to see. Sometimes there was a moon and stars and God was close by. Floating among the clouds was the dream of wife, sweetheart, family and home – where they ought to be.

Just as suddenly, the horror was over. Circumstances again not anticipated and again no choice to make. Comrades who have lived and died in belief of one another do not change. It was not strange that distance parted comrades but comrades of others were not strangers but buddies now. There was a growing legion of newly bonded buddies in command. The intricacies of a newfound culture – it was the world that changed again.

The "Males Only Bar" featured a cherished player piano. The haunting theme "My Buddy" was a just released piano roll so often heard, a solemn toast to days gone by. The rousing *"How 'Ya Gonna Keep 'Em Down on the Farm (After They've Seen Paree)?"* was on a record in the corner machine.

Network Radio was the music on the left: "Stardust," Paul Whiteman or the theme song of a guitar band played. Prospering merchants featured weekend "Thank You, Soldier" sales with an extra discount to a veteran. Sunday concerts in the town square and smiling people everywhere. "The Roaring Twenties," Hot Jazz, radios and cars – Al Capone and G-men and fun – "American" the vibrant life, as known nowhere else.

There was also the unreal, that ever-zooming stock market. Shoeshine guys were new millionaires in paper shares. Air mail, telephones and Model T Fords. The world of progress that would never end – but it did.

The zooming stock market fell and people panicked. The cruel and ever-fickle fates had proven once again that man is born, that means he is alive. Destiny is not a birthright but a happening – it is: chance, circumstance, opportunity and associates that control.

The human impact, the tragedies of life, bitter memories that fade in the need of "To Forget." The damaged veteran once paid homage, now knows rejection. Payment of the bonus once firmly promised was then forgotten. The Peaceful March for Justice met federal troops (their former comrades in battle) under orders to resist. The general in command (a leader that they had bravely followed) now ordered "Fire at will" if they do not promptly disperse. It was the spirit if not the soul of the nation that was under threat of fire that day. Someone somewhere had so ordered – But Who and Why?

CHAPTER ELEVEN

WHERE DID ALL THE GOOD TIMES GO?

"Neither times nor substance can be destroyed, hence do all things revert to whence they came?"

The chronicle of transition within those many yesterdays does not relate to points of departure but axial periods of advancing knowledge of the earth in form and format. Man's relationship with fellow man and contrasting philosophies develop. Pay proper homage to all in any test of progress.

One cannot swim in the same river twice. What has been done is forever etched in the indelible marks of time just as individual conscience and instincts are finely honed. Everyone lives within one's self but survives within the structured disciplines of the common good. The so-called Dark Age is conveniently tagged the great unknown, where time and matter held no meaning. Genesis, the first book of the Bible, portrays a point of origin, the creation of the planet Earth. Within this text, the Ten Commandments dictated the first rules of law. The promise of redemption was to be served in the coming of a Messiah that would mark a new beginning, the Year of the Lord. A so-called Period of Enlightenment as defined in the Philosophies of Aristotle precedes the Birth of Christ, the stem of Christianity, by some 3 centuries. The Sermon on the Mount and the New Testament of the Bible and the Judeo Christian precept was avowed.

Heritage is honored as human failure intrudes, ambitions preclude a stagnant world. The challenge of men to lead other men has haunted all civilizations since time began. Countless theologies have coined expressions in contrast, often conflict, with the obligations of the culture that derives. As so nurtured, this culture framed a constitution predicated on the precept of the individual and his creator.

Any generation is the product of those many yesterdays, the bedrock of commitment, but the reality of now demands specifics that truly reflect the temperament of the day. This Nation was not conceived through compromise but the pragmatic of good and evil – right and wrong and the conviction of those who led and the many that will follow. This is what the "Good Times" are. Where the go is never far away, lurking always in the wings. A new day is found in the fires from where we came.

Those near yesterdays, in which the world was falsely known, suppression was control. Man's inhumanity to fellow man as Nations warred in hollow cause as ignorance and persecution was the way of life. Skip to century fifteen, know that before then the world was as but a flat plane around which the sun evolved and gravity was of no concern.

Half the world away, was another land, there too it may have been thought the world was flat. This land had been created and then placed in limbo not reserve. Protected from the eastern sphere by an expanse of ocean, the west was not yet known to exist. Two continents formed along a global line – north and south. All lands in eons past but for reason never known the western sphere was left alone – or was it the sphere that moved?

The if, when, and how the earth was settled is not topical here, pre-historic ruins confirm an ancient occupancy and depicts a developing culture not unlike the pursuits of our own. The absence of a document does not suggest there is no history nor that one pre-dates the other. Two hemispheres, each cloistered from the other by forbidding turbulent expanses of water. These hemispheres did not coexist but existed simultaneously.

CHAPTER TWELVE

THIS IS HOW WE GOT HERE

A talented Italian named Columbus, blessed with courage, somehow charmed the Queen of Spain – that by sailing west the riches of the east were waiting to be brought to Spain. She sold her jewels. She bought his dream. It was she who found that the earth was part of a planet now proven to be round, not flat.

Three small ships, ill equipped, poorly crewed and sparsely provisioned – by chance encountered the Western Hemisphere. He landed on an island in a calm, blue sea and there were people there.

The year was 1492

Columbus was welcomed by the happy natives – the antics of his motley crew met firm rejection. It was a tribal law all things shared, in a land of plenty all things were free. He named the sea, Caribbean as it came to be known, the many nearby islands and the mainland just beyond. The primitive, happy people of origin unknown were soon to know the harsh rule of Spain.

True to the lusts of conquest and the lure of souls to save – the salvation of America was launched in massive numbers. The Gospel of Rome, the Signet of Madrid, conquerors in full armor and monks in the hooded garb or cincture habit to spread the word of Rome and the rule of Spain. The spread was rapid, from the mainland; west on the wide river, now known as the Rio Grande, was secure. A cultured population had been conquered, they were in awe of the horses they had never seen before. It was decided by those Balboa had left to rule to establish a government center in the highland city they had occupied. They called it Mexico.

The Year was 1513 AD

Balboa had ventured farther south conquering and converting all along the way. The land veered to the east. He elected to continue to the south. It was a narrow strip of land and there was a vast ocean beyond. He named it Pacific.

The year was 1516 AD

Spanish conquest pursued to the south, there was a continent beyond. History had awarded all lands explored by Balboa to Colonial Spain.

CHAPTER THIRTEEN

THE AMERICAS

One North – One South

All territory north was otherwise left to be explored by France and England who were in conflict once again, or more correctly, still.

Somewhere within the range of birth to death is a point or time where reason is achieved. The forming of this nation scribes a scale of points and shifting modes but forever constant. The precepts and purpose of freedom and liberty avowed. Nations are not born in the sense of created life but physically formulated in response to man's need for rule. The strength of will and basic logic motivate the dedication and disciplines of survival.

"Freedom," a wishful phrase, was conceived in the ideal hopes of those condemned to the abuse of royal rule – generations who could only dream.

"Liberty" as a reality found birth in the virgin lands to the west where loyalty to the crown persisted and fear and of the past was dimmed. Years of struggle had straightened attitudes and confidence. Later immigrants brought a higher learning and fostered a lust for knowledge in those already here. The colonials were "better read" and "better informed" than their contemporaries in the more sophisticated continental clime.

A proud new nation reflects the intellect and dedication

of those we honor as our founders. Be aware that all success was at a high cost in blood and sacrifice of countless thousands in the centuries since men first recognized the need of rule and then knew its abuse.

The French and Indian Wars had been costly in blood and fortune to both the colonies and the crown. Washington had devoted affiliations with some Indian tribes but many remained attached to the defeated French. The crown when faced with a depleted treasury was attentive to the increasing wealth within the colonies. The jealous and clumsy British Parliament levied oppressive high taxes on all colonial commerce. Import duties on goods shipped from the continent and essential to survival were resented most. Attempts to arbitrate were rudely rejected by the Parliament. Attempts to communicate directly to the crown were ignored. The proud and justified colonies declared their Independence, July 4, 1776.

"These are the days that try men's souls"

– The opening lines from an Essay by Thomas Paine.

It was the harsh winter of 1776 that found Washington and his troops retreating across the Delaware in defeat. The war had not gone well; had the nation acted in haste?

The Essay speaks of the needs of a Nation something more than Summer Soldiers and Sunshine Patriots.

It was a bitter time that questioned, gave doubts that the American experience ever would succeed. The nature of that experience is of historical and social merit. For the first time in history a nation was being brought into being not through debates and resolutions but by a group that found unity in a cause and purpose. They all, well and widely read but at the same time practical, were determined and courageous.

All had studied Montesque's "Spirit of The Laws" which discussed the different sense of responsibility that had to develop depending on the regime under which people will live. The capacity for fear in a monarchy, a capacity for liberty, the taste of honor, a republic cast in the virtue of rights endowed.

The Spanish Empire, a conquest too distant to control; Venezuela, Columbia Ecuador, Peru and Bolivia once viceroys, now sovereign entities, The Bolivar Constitution avowed in collective rights, in lieu of papal rule. There was no common purpose – no mutual dedication, no individual concerns but a central control. The divide of Europe by empire was mimicked in greater error and lesser form.

Thirteen sovereign colonies in sharp contrast, were dedicated to the cause of individual liberty. Each separately chartered strictly cloistered, fiercely independent yet each had found greater strength in a unity of purpose.

A confederation of sovereign states, now a sovereign nation – states united and so governed under consent of those governed "All men are created equal endowed by their Creator."

A Lone Figure – a flickering campfire. A consuming sense of prayer, the terrors of the day, the haunt of violent death. There were military tents in precise rows behind. Exhausted yet sleepless, survivors …Why?... Shared emotions, stifled sobs – the solemn interchange that their silence conveys. The black night and hostile skies mirrored the conflicts of the troubled time and mourned the cost in blood and tears. The

“’Lone Figure” was sheltered from the bitter cold by a military cape that bore the marks of rank – his posture wore the stamp of leader. The Continental Army had but one they followed. George Washington was alone not in the solitude of self-pity but in appraisal of reality when faced with what is real.

Brave men in shock, zombies in crowded tents and many more for whom there were no tents. Exhausted, battle-hardened troops who knew nightmares now and would never know a happy dream again. They had followed him the days before – only glory in their mind – soon bullets flew and comrades fell, some not to rise again. Mangled bodies, twisted thoughts, the only mission was to stay alive but instincts controlled. He had taught them to survive but there is no teaching them how to forget: “His troops,” war and courage, “The Continental Congress,” Revolution and Purpose. Valor forged with dedication cast the dye that changed the world of “His Compatriots.”

Other brave men defiant – challenging the crown –

“We mutually pledge to each other our lives, our fortunes and our sacred honor.”

Washington did not grieve in the solitude of a vacant conscience or in false compassion. Lives, sacrificed were a tribute to the cause, no guilt, no comfort in the dying fire – no pardon in the coming dawn. The Revolution was ignited by betrayals long before. Sovereign colonies, loyal subjects – abused by Parliament then to know the harsh rebuff, the cruelty, of the crown.

The stench of sweat, the stain of blood, the smell of death was too familiar, too deeply etched in memory. The French and Indian War was a laboratory in military tactics and lessons in the conflict of Ideals – but the education of George Washington was his comprehension of individuals, their rights and the honor of human values.

His early days were spent on the frontier, accompanied if not guarded, by British soldiers as he surveyed the boundaries of the Massachusetts Bay Colony. He had made friends with the few Indians who did not show contempt. He had learned respect, if not envy, of the pragmatic culture and structured codes of behavior of a functioning society of the ill-termed "Savages."

The mystery of untamed lands both attracted and repelled the challenge of silence in the turmoil of nature in the wild. These extremes of environs do not sculpture the range of majesty, the glory that entrapped the shifting glories in the skies. The compensating demands of nature were easily ignored, life casually defined as death delayed. Cleared and cultivated areas not invasions, not shelters but enhancements of the land. Wilderness the source of wild game was also a barrier of protection and other elements of survival.

Washington mastered sign language, some English words were learned by Indians – communication was achieved. Washington mimicked the French fur traders in cultivating Indian relations. He learned that a tree was a protective friend, a shelter when attacked, concealment in the hunt for food – not just a place to hide. Each Indian pursues the mission as an individual involved in a common cause. Contrast this with massed troops that meet in combat in an open field each intent on the slaughter of the other – the conventions of the so-termed "Civilized." Does this project a bravado of courage or a code of lesser morals? The term "savage" rightly applies to whom?

Ever-increasing violence by rogue tribes and errant French trappers demanded retaliation, ultimately the costly war spanned some six years. French trade destroyed, colonial militias were tested and excelled. Empire mercenaries were introduced and the cruelty of British regulars was too often needless. The contempt and frustration of British officers was disclosed as their human and material resources drained. Victory was a vacant word, France had lost but what had the empire won? It was only the colonials that advanced in unity and confidence.

Indian tactics mastered had dominated the range of combat, the conduct of attack. The successful scaling of the unguarded heights of Quebec, the defeat of the French. It was the colonial militias and Indian tactics that had controlled the wild.

George Washington was the symbol of the Independence that was declared, leadership not rhetoric but purpose.

CHAPTER FOURTEEN

THE BIRTH OF A NATION

"We the People"

"...in Order to form a more perfect Union, establish Justice, insure domestic Tranquility, provide for the common defence, promote the general Welfare, and secure the Blessings of Liberty to ourselves and our Posterity, do ordain and establish this Constitution..."

An adventure in Human Endeavor
The Envy of the World

"Human Endeavor" the nuptial of ideal with purpose – the force of will with the energy of moral cause. The Declaration of Independence solemnly avows this principle, "All Men are created equal endowed by their Creator with certain unalienable Rights." The governing of men as administered by men demands a government strong enough to control the people yet not inhibit their freedom and yet stranger still, to control itself. Any semblance of royal rule as associated with divine right is refuted. Assuring all disciplines of control and the dignity of each Sovereign Colony had been a perplexing challenge. This concern was of first address in earliest meetings of the proposed Confederation.

The Constitution of the United States is forged in the

noble proclamation of The Declaration of Independence. It is tempered in text and fundamentals by the Petition of Right and the English Bill of Rights and Precedents of the British Parliament.

Freedom within Order -
Equality within Reason
"Rights Endowed a Legacy of Trust"

Acknowledge the foresight of the unchallenged but not yet accepted, Continental Congress directed that a convention be convened. It was charged with the task of drafting a Constitution, to be presented for congressional approval then submission to the thirteen colonies for ratification. Delegates were appointed by each of the colonies; the convention convened in Philadelphia in the late 1780s.

Reflect on the floundering delegates striving to suppress their individual interests in hope for harmony with the delegates of other states in the sacrifice of sovereignty to a national authority (73 delegates were appointed, only 55 ever appeared). Everyone in the steamy Convention Hall was constantly cognizant that the government that they were structuring would succeed or fail to the extent that it enjoyed the consent of the governed. Appeal had to be at a level that an average citizen could easily understand and that advantages so well explained that no known alternative would work so well. Respect the talents of compromising

– the surrender of state sovereignty to a national authority – reconciling major differences between states in the governing parametric – the jealousies and differing vanities of individual delegates was the challenge. To resolve the limits and powers of the central government was the purpose and the demand. The autonomy of the thirteen colonies accommodating the ever-expanding frontiers and the rapidly increasing population was the further task. The urgency of forming a formal system of government was the objective.

Bickering faded in the face of challenge posed by gifted leaders. "Why are we here?" A singular response of individual intent and purpose and nature of demand as was agreement to the surrender of colony severity, and recognition of central control, as limited in structure and scope. Increasing delegate awareness that unity in common purpose was essential, that defined in a single sentence was the resolution – words etched in commitment and guaranty. The Prelude – introducing the three independent branches of government and the powers specifically granted and vested to each.

Through the long hours and many days of discourse, bitter memories of the abuses of British rule and parliamentary arrogance were an obsession of many and retained by all. Final drafts of the Articles of Confederation delineated three separate branches of government and specifically detailed the functions vested in each. Fearful of a weak separation each from the other was the cause of continuing concern. These fears were quieted through the energy and efforts principally of Hamilton and Madison. The full draft (signed by 39 delegates) was recommended and passed to the Congress for their approval. Be aware of the dedication and talents of the delegates and the energy demands in view of growing fatigue. The resulting Constitution is neither a perfect document nor an exercise in philosophy but one of agreement and acceptance of those so governed. Never before in history had a government been structured to the equality of all and rights endowed to the individual as natures law entitles him. This recognition of rights and freedom is our nation.

The process of congressional approval again addressed concerns on a most positive separation of what is to occur, powers vested in the three branches of government. The early admonitions of John Adams were recalled "Human nature know thyself." Should the power to legislate reside within the power to judge – tyranny will shortly follow." The fear of an ambitious judiciary was much discussed, concurred rather than debated. "Deny the purse/Deny the sword" – a definition of an independent judiciary in the negative, and dependence on the jealous stewardship specifically vested powers was the resolution, hopefully not to be a later concern.

Direct address to the Articles of Confederation "Bill of Rights" was absolutely essential for congressional approval and ratification by the states. Recognizing the folly of listing individual rights in any possible entirety, it was determined that central government restrictions be detailed. The scope of central authority is documented – Amendments 1 through 10.

The absolute is that time appointed, that date with destiny, the point of transition from the subjective of hopes and dreams to the reality of intent, guaranty and practice. The personal emotion in the inauguration of George Washington as repeated so many times. Often overlooked but of equal consequence in the transition was the dedication of those elected or appointed their pledge to service and commitment in conscience and performance.

The Federalist and Anti-Federalist Papers were further

attentive to the transition of the Articles of Confederation to a central authority. Be ever mindful of Amendments 1 thru 10 "The Bill of Rights" as essential to ratification by the original thirteen states. " "We the People"," rights not dedicated to central authority are retained by the state or the individual. Limited government, states rights versus central government. Sovereignty, the ultimate assurance.

Government by The Governed
How Long Can It Endure?

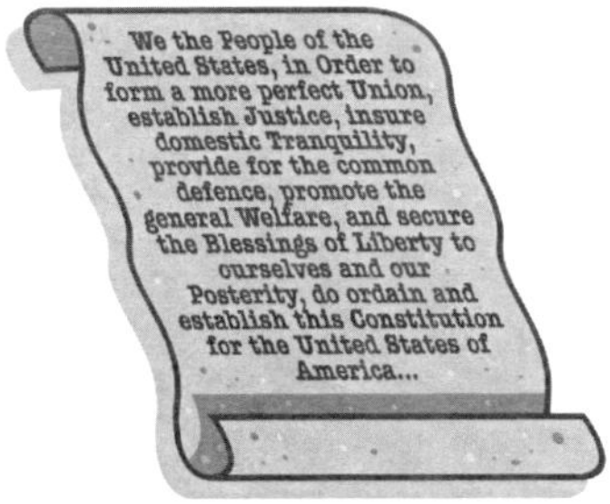

CHAPTER FIFTEEN

THE WAR OF 1812

No name, no glory just remembered for what it was: "The war declared by someone else." Battles were many and widely spread, none were named but mementos survive. Francis Scott Key found honor under British fire in Baltimore Harbor, Fort McHenry is not on a foreign shore. The Star Spangled Banner was written there and it contains two more verses seldom sung or heard. Admiral Perry's "We have just begun to fight," it was spoken on Lake Erie, not some distant sea. Tories who had fled to Canada joined British scouts to harass, not openly attack. New York was threatened; the White House sacked and burned; they then withdrew.

A British flotilla penetrated the Gulf; the Mississippi River was the goal. The land forded forces of which General Jackson lacked ability to defend. It was ships of the Pirate Empire that knew Gulf winds and shores. The British Admiral chose wisely not to fight and thus sailed south, then east. Jean Lafitte, the pirate leader, is still honored in New Orleans; do all tourists know the reason why?

General Jackson awakened to the strategic location Florida, a Spanish colony that controlled the Gulf coast from the confluence of three states and the river basin. Pirate enclaves controlled the many islands and the waters of the Gulf.

The interest of the day was run-away slaves who had escaped to Florida via Atlantic waters from Georgia and the

Carolinas and overland through Alabama. The escapees easily adapted to the humidity, heat and insects of the swamps and had organized in peaceful settlements, their safety well protected by natural hazards that only they knew how to survive. Jackson thought it better to return north, the hero that he was sure he was. "Old Hickory" was a title that his home town newspaper had bestowed. The popularity of Old Hickory did not fade, it filled a void in a period of listless wander, half slave – half free. The Federal Courts were no help.

Elected President in 1828 he did not shirk the task. His Inaugural Address, one of the shortest ever, solemnly pledged to the nation his zealous dedication to the service of their good, strict accountability of their revenues, fair administration of their laws and the conduct of foreign and Confederate relations.

Most Significant was the repeated reference to the sanctity and dedication to the Constitution, the sovereignty of individual states and their equality in federal assets. The army and navy were separate units of defense to be funded separately and so managed.

His best judgment was, "An armed militia of one million men is the guarantee of the security of the Nation." There was no question, what he meant. The stuffy culture of Washington and the formal White House was exposed to the uninhibited behavior of the frontier; they learned to live with it. Andrew Jackson was not a hero to many but still survived. He was elected to a second term in 1832.

CHAPTER SIXTEEN

THE CIVIL WAR

A convenient conscience, suppressed honor and principles betrayed. It is from this base line that faults are measured and penance unfolds

Greed and bigotry had taken hold, there is little difference – north or south – ethics forgotten, all conscience suppressed. The words equality, freedom and liberty now in conflict – political expediency controlled – the Constitution betrayed. Corruption was the product, the maturing nation found decay. A bleak horizon can shade but not destroy the scales of justice – that certain sun will rise, a new day will unfold, all penalties will be paid.

The Christian clergy in the north found a unity of conscience in a belated recognition of their past failure to denounce the horrors of servitude, the sacrilege of denial. Homilies in wealthy congregations strongly condemned slavery in the cotton fields but failed to mention the depraved working conditions in Massachusetts mills and the factories in New York. The words were lost; the pompous rich went to church to be seen, not to hear a sermon. They all hummed "John Brown's Body" the favorite tune of the day and read "Uncle Tom's Cabin" the favorite book. Sympathy was hollow, empathy found tears, few hearts, far less remorse.

The poor at prayer in smaller churches, there was no homily, no common language; most came from lands apart.

They were in church to pray for better days. They too were slaves, but did not know the word or what it meant. They could not read, they had no time to sing nor anything to sing about.

Churches in the south were different; slaves went to church with their master, whites in private pews, blacks in the crowded loft. They sang the all hymns, together. Happiness and peace a constant atmosphere on the contented plantation but it was an era of moral denial destined to be avenged.

Newly developed areas were the scene of greed and cruelty, the curse that accompanied the decline of that era of shame. Resentment and revenge brewed in the hovels that slaves were condemned to in these infested lands.

Slaves were bought and sold without regard for families, husband, wife or child. There was much that was "wrong." Slave masters, at casual whim, made black maidens concubines to increase their inventory of slaves. Mulattos were condemned to the quarter. Why not the mansion? They are half-white. Can anything be judged in moral terms when it is immorality that is at stake?

Cruelty and abuse became the common practice, as more depraved alleged humans owned slaves. Soon the self-consuming culture crumbled, humanity on the wings of fate prevailed. Political partners found a fertile field and newspapers found a way to expand circulation. The passions and emotions of a nation that had slumbered far too long were aroused and blind ignorance reacted. Abolitionists in the north vied with Separatists in the south both bent on destruction of the Union. Vanity was the lure, states' rights the slogans but slavery was the cause. The Constitution had been betrayed, the wrath of God awaited.

Agriculture, cotton gins and the industries in Birmingham, Alabama, were the total assets of the south. Steel mills, foundries and factories were among the industrial asset of the north. A navy, population and immigration were the dominating physical assets of the north. Blood and sacrifice the cost to each, always paid by someone else.

The Underground Railroad, stealth and danger – slaves

found freedom. A romantic story but the secret stops of hidden peril, the steps of terror; it was an adventure claimed by many but the horror of the trail was the triumph of a valiant few.

Blood was shed and many died before the Confederacy was formed. Bigotry found foe, there was no issue, just where you went to church or where you used to live. Kansas Jay Hawks ravaged Missouri outskirts claiming to avenge the slaves but the ravaged never owned one. Missouri bands avenged the raid, men died before they were told why. Military leaders of the south claimed early victories but the industrial capacity, depth of manpower gained final victory for the Union. The war of highest loss in human life was fought between brothers, even father versus son. The north and south both survived. They had suffered as a nation, the Union saved at a cost far too high – the wasted, the dead-memories fade but never die.

The Civil War did not end with military surrender or a sudden return to tranquility, but an extended period of national shame. The defeated south was plundered by northern carpetbaggers. They confiscated the property of those whose crops and lands had been wantonly tilled by battles from

Vicksburg to Savannah. The cotton mills of Massachusetts and the factories throughout New England condoned cruelty, the match of slavery. Indentured immigrants were abused as greed flourished. Children and adults of any age braved ovens in summer, freezers in winter to survive. Dust filled stagnant air, the day was long – some died before the sun set but the suffering of others knew no end.

A once-divided nation is slow to reunite. Abraham Lincoln, the savior, was assassinated before healing could begin. The nation was without a leader, denied the empathy of his feeling soul. His words of true peace "with malice toward none and charity for all" were hollow, he was succeeded by lesser men. The defeated south suffered far too much and far too long.

Vice-President Johnson took office at the death of Lincoln. He met active resistance and petty attack. He was falsely impeached but found not guilty; it was not the nation's finest hour.

Legacy of Conflict, the price of change.

General Grant, the war hero, was the next elected president; his popularity was concentrated in the northern states. The war-ravaged south had only bitter memories of the Union Army and he was the general. The military culture was the only life he knew. This did not fully qualify him for the normal duties of the office; he was further challenged in the aftermath of rebellion. Half the nation was without hope – half on the brink of post-war prosperity, a nation devoid of empathy, possessed by greed and loss of heart and soul. He was obsessed with the war-driven national debt but more attentive to the poverty and plunder now suffered in the defeated south that a living Lincoln had so well addressed. He was an early advocate of suffrage; his inaugural address encouraged early enactment of the pending 15th Amendment. "A portion of the citizens of the nation should not be excluded from its privileges." President Grant served two terms during a turbulent period of recovery, transition and economic disturbance. His term of office expired in the midst of the Depression. Never honoring his mastery of a still-divided people, he was critically judged by the fickle American press. His reputation was the symbol of United States Prestige in Foreign Lands - But overlooked At Home.

CHAPTER SEVENTEEN

THE NATION MATURES

Increasingly hostile contact was expected with an ever-restless Mexico in the south and brief but intense disciplinary incursions were a recurring task of American cavalry. The north was blessed with constant peace. The Monroe Doctrine was the declared the nation's foreign policy. Such was the American image in the closing days of the 19th century.

Spain had lost all control in South America as revolts led by Simon Bolivar and other adventurers were successful. The once proud colonial empire was reduced to a few scattered missions too small to be known in Madrid. The major islands in the Caribbean were military outposts but the troops were listless restless, the populace resistless. United States involvement was not openly invited but secretly entertained. The obsolete battleship USS Maine was sunk with loss of life, not in open attack but in suspicious circumstance. The United States was at war with Spain.

A long-lasting legacy of Spain was the genetic aspects of the Spanish language and a continuing enforcement of its singular acceptance in all legal transactions. The unification influence of a language had lasting impact in the western world; the Spanish language united the western hemisphere with the single common tongue where bullets failed. Bilingual realities pose only division and distrust, not inherent but cultivated. The ability to communicate is an essential of existence and the melding of differing cultures. This reality is demonstrated in the geography of Europe and the history of conflicts therein. The Western Hemisphere is far less divided. The previously mentioned Spanish language influence has captured all but Brazil of Portuguese loyalty, and the United States and Canada (excepting French in Quebec). Where English was the common language and a predicate of citizenship. The newly established territories in the southwest petitioning statehood were subject to and accepted this criterion.

Cuba was the area of initial contest; the charge of San Juan Hill by the Rough Riders, a cavalry force led by a political favorite, Teddy Roosevelt, captured the glory and immortalized "Teddy" the leader.

The Spanish America War was a lesser war but most significant as a point of transition in world domination.

The liberation of Cuba signaled the ending of Spanish influence in the Caribbean and any lingering loyalty to Madrid. A conquest too distant to control; no way to defend. The colonial empire of proud Spain collapsed. The United States was proclaimed a world power, 1898.

The nation was alive. American and Canadian interests were a single force; sea level canals, the Erie and the Wellend, bypassing Niagara Falls, connecting the Great Lakes and the Atlantic Ocean. The energies of the region now accessible, 1904, prosperity was hypnotic. Teddy Roosevelt, President of the United States. The electorate unaware of a Progressive agenda. An elitist political culture now controlled and destined for longer life.

CHAPTER EIGHTEEN

THE PANAMA CANAL

The Panama Canal is indelibly linked to Teddy Roosevelt's foresight and his particular talents. The canal was not a new idea nor a venture of unknown difficulties. The Isthmus of Panama was a fifty-mile strip of jungle growth, mosquitoes, reptiles and varying elevations; fever-ridden humid climate and all other discomforts known to man, but a physical miracle separating the awesome and opposing energies of the Atlantic and Pacific Oceans. This narrow land mass alternatively enabled the convenient and economical interchange of commerce from ocean to ocean and north to south. The intrinsic value of this infested piece of real estate had been recognized at the time of discovery of the Pacific Ocean and first exploited in the overland transfer of Peruvian riches to Spain.

Ferdinand de Lesseps of Suez Canal fame had organized a commercial venture to construct a canal connecting the two great oceans. The glamour appeal of the venture ignored the complexities of the tropics. A jungle to conquer, a mountain to scale, constant rain but worst of all was fever and death. Some five years of miss-adventure ended in admitted failure, a financial disaster that crippled a nation. Contemptuous of failures of others in the past, the new administration recovered the abandoned equipment and applied common sense. The health hazards were of first concern: potable water, sewage disposal, fever control, personnel security and logistic stability were the challenges first faced. An abundance of fresh water and the technologies perfected in conjunction with the influx of visitors to the World's Fair in St. Louis lessened water supply concerns. The French venture had constructed dock facilities and a rustic rail line from coast to coast that could be enhanced, relieving logistics concerned. A Lieutenant-Colonel Russell Elliott Wood of the Army Medical Corps had established the mosquito as a prime conduit in the spread of yellow fever, the first cousin of all fevers. His policies of absolute sanitation and the elimination of stagnant water accumulation were accepted as the policy to be rigidly enforced.

The isthmus, an acknowledged appendage of the northwestern extremity of South America, was within the borders of the Republic of Columbia. Aware that this remote territory was open to attack and realizing that sovereignty had been compromised in the de Lesseps adventure, the United States was now protective of this valued territory. The United States envoy in Bogotá was advised of Columbian interest in the cooperation with the United States in the development of a canal, but only on the basis of joint and equal sovereignty over the isthmus. The United States was to assume all costs of construction and of territorial security, the canal to be under joint Republic of Columbia and United States operation and control.

Somewhere within the state department or the White House, communication ceased. Columbian officials in Panama City declared the isthmus free and independent, all ties to the Republic of Columbia to cease in 1903. The United States immediately recognized the Republic of Panama. By some unknown stroke, the Republic of Panama tendered a ninety-nine-year lease covering a north-to-south six-mile strip, of the Republic land for the sole purpose of constructing a connecting canal, Atlantic to Pacific Oceans. This action in total was the product of ineptitude unmatched in deceit and betrayal of responsibilities. The nation was shielded, shame submerged.

The Panama Canal, a Wonder of The World, ships moved north and south through those fifty miles, an international asset, 1913. Triumph of medical and engineering genius is a living tribute to the talents and energy of the United States; it is rightly said that no other nation is so blessed. An ever-haunting shadow clouds the isthmus of some fifty miles, it hovers closest a six-mile strip of steamy, snake and insect ridden festering jungle that surrounds it.

A six-mile strip, not the geography, but the coined morality. A ninety-nine-year lease of disillusion. The genius of design, the medical talent, construction skills, the energy of the nation; a lasting Wonder of the World.

The Canal, two oceans joined…

Atlantic Locks at Colon, Gillard Cut and Gatun Lake.

Miraflores Lake

Pacific Locks at Balboa, Pedro Miguel and Miraflores

CHAPTER NINETEEN

PROGRESS OR DECAY

Pride in achievements of the re-constituted Union was well merited but euphoria was hallowing as apathy betrayed. The conscience of the nation was submerged, the Constitution was under siege. Government in false function maybe just exists.

The Constitution is not in parallel but in conflict with Progressivism; the stakes mirror the cancer of progress as exposed to decay – ideology and commitment cannot survive in harmony; only one survives.

From Many One

The measure of time and the reality of human suffering are individually endured, the horror in memory there dies and vengeance fades. History pays homage to the transitions in the power of nations and the physical attributes that were attendant. The evils that led to Civil War, and then claimed a price the nation has yet to atone, the nation still struggles to assign the faults that continue to accrue. The burden of performance, the cost of enduring peace, the penalties of liberties surrendered was not equally assessed and still then unknown.

Be ever alert to things no longer mentioned that warped the purity of our founding. It was the abrupt misgiving of the Dred Scott decision that nurtured the resentments the structure of the Constitution had intended to avoid. Man's inhumanity to man was the curse of generations long before the Western

Hemisphere was known to exist, and that slavery was in practice there that were elsewhere unknown. Massive injustice and individual cruelties can be immediately curtailed, punishment assessed but the disaster of dependence must be cured and the dependent taught to survive.

The slaves in the more Northern Colonies were more like indentured servants, be they in the field or in the house. All completely dependent on the master for the necessities of life and anything beyond – most mistreated, but they were not free. As a culture, slave practice was in ever-loosing favor, it was mainly the obligations of dependence that controlled. Many blacks were patriots; the hero of the battle of Bunker Hill was black. Observe that famous paintings commemorating the war portrayed black faces in the troops. It was intended that the functions of the Constitution provide the path to "all men are created equal." As truth demands, compromise is doomed to fail. The Civil War was the result.

Cotton and sugar controlled the lifestyle in the south, manual labor was the demand and slavery was the response; there was no other source and had historically served the need. The immigration of slaves was outlawed in 1809 to assuage the conscience of the nation but the judicial action – declaring humans to be the property of another – was in condemnation.

The futility of compromise, there is no negotiation, no balancing when the test is right from wrong. The Missouri Compromise was truth betrayed, the nation to be no longer united – no longer "From the many one." The greed of the north in contest with the greed of the south, the nation that could not live, half slave/half free." A Civil War, a spirit died – no hope, time to reconcile. A hollow victory and the tragedy of defeat to haunt a vacant sky – the Progressive Movement found an open gate.

The victorious north experienced a far less stressful period of post-war recovery. Westward expansion and industrial development in the Great Lakes region, aided by productive immigration, brought slow but steady economic benefit. Political intrigue was a constant wave of change. It was the war with Spain that formally proclaimed the nation's power. The political dominance of the progressive thrust in political, social and economic policies was declared in the election of Teddy Roosevelt as president in 1904. He and political Progressivism were in context and in perfect harmony but Teddy, always a disruptive force, was bored. The Orient had captured his next ambition; a second term would interfere. William Howard Taft, his political ward, failed him by lacking energy for the Progressive agenda. He soon lost favor. The vain and ever-ambitious Roosevelt was again divisive. He formed the Bull Moose, a third party to oppose Taft and the Democrat candidate in the election of 1912.

The Republican electorate was split. Woodrow Wilson, a Democrat Progressive, was elected in default, his radicalism was extensive. Wilson, a taciturn elitist, was re-elected to a second term on the promise to keep us "Out of War." American troops landed in France within weeks of planned betrayal. Amendments Sixteen through Eighteen were the products of his wild ambition in a nation that had been manipulated through an impotent Congress and then ratified by an apathetic public. He had little interest in the conduct of war but was obsessed with the process of armistice and to subjugate the nation in his personal fantasy of "One World." He was credited or more properly charged as being a principle author of the Versailles Peace Treaty.

United States involvement in the League of Nations was wisely rejected and failed Congressional approval. The destructive Versailles Treaty was the platform that first gave

Adolph Hitler power and the basic cause of World War II. The treaty that Jack Kennedy later referred to forty years hence as "That Harsh and Bitter Peace."

Wilson's final weeks in offices were a blank; illness prevented public appearance and he denied contact to all but his closest advisors. His wife was the closest of all. The Madam Wilson was cold and unyielding, it was she who was the president those final days before he died. A ruptured Constitution his legacy, a now more troubled nation was to pay a heavy price.

The Progressive Movement had lost all public appeal with the unpopularity of Woodrow Wilson and the deep economic decline in the last years of his administration. The demise of Wilson prompted a new identity for the movement, The term Liberal was applied.

The magnitude and impact of the three Constitutional Amendments that were created and ratified in the four presidential terms of progressive adventure:

Hijacked the interaction and structuring of the House and Senate. (Amendment 16)

A Federal Income Tax to be directly imposed on individual incomes confiscated prerogative reserved to the States. (Amendment 17)

Social norms and individual behavior was captivated then awarded to a cult of bigotry (Amendment 18)

The Constitution of the United States of America has ruled for some 220 years. It is the oldest- ever written, nation/state constitution in constant operation. A marvel of brevity, as amended 27 times, it totals just 7606 words. The sports section of today's newspaper contains far more words of far less import.

The founders recognized that the Constitution would require periodic alteration so they included an Amending Article 5, which requires the consent of both federal and state governments to amend the Constitution. As an alternative to the action of both Houses of Congress in proposing amendments, the application of two thirds of the legislatures several states shall call a convention for proposing amendments.

The greatest concern of Anti-Federalist was then a Supremacy Clause Article 6, Section 2 (the Role of the Supreme Court). This led to a Bill of Rights (extracted from the abandoned Articles of Confederation) added as Amendments 1 thru 10 the Constitution as submitted by the Congress for Ratification. (March 4, 1789). Ten of the twelve were approved as the Bill of Rights; affirmation by the State of New York achieved the required majority and the Constitution so ratified in 1791.

Amendment 10 is climactic in that it places restrictions on government, not individuals. "The powers not delegated to the United States by the Constitution, nor prohibited by it to the states, are reserved to the states respectively or to the people."

Amendments 1, 4 and 6 reflect powers prohibited to the government by the Constitution.

Amendments 5 and 8 reflect powers reserved to the people.

Amendments 2, 3, 7 and 9 reflect powers reserved to the states.

Amendments 11 through 15 were ratified through the period ending 1870.

Seventeen amendments were subsequently ratified and altered the method for selecting the president. Six amendments have extended the voting franchise. Two amendments (13, 18) have been ratified reflecting change in social values. Three amendments have been added to overcome Supreme Court rulings: Amendment 11 (Chisom vs. Georgia), Amendment 14 (Dred Scott) and Amendment 16 (Income Tax).

Amendment 19 (ratified August 18, 1920) is of particular interest:

"The right of citizens of the United States to vote shall not be denied abridged by the United States or any State on account of sex."

Women were granted voting rights – seven months later the Carrie Nations, a woman's group intent on curbing the use of liquor, ceased destroying mahogany bars in corner saloons.

The presidential election of 1924 was a repudiation of the Democratic Party in the name of Wilson. A strong pro-business, low-tax Republican platform captivated a despondent nation. Warren Harding the president, his personal failures were too late disclosed. His when and from where did freedom stem?

Shortened term featuring turpitude merited spousal friction. Vice-President Calvin Coolidge, his absolute opposite, ascended to the office in the best definition of transition. His rigid adherence was to the principles of the platform that led to his election. The 1920's depression was short lived. Coolidge was elected to a full term in 1924 but did not choose to run for what could be considered a third term.

The "Roaring Twenties," the post-war economic attribute that had been delayed through the turbulent Wilson agenda, was a testimony of the Coolidge economic disciplines and low tax policies. The excesses and lavish lifestyle was attributable to the aftermath of the war. The fantasy of prohibition was the cradle of the era of debauchery that followed. The legacy of that criminal culture still roams free today.

Herbert Hoover, a Republican, was not true to his campaign promises. He reverted to the policies avowed by the entrenched bureaucracies, a legacy of the of the Wilson days. Free market commitment that he had professed was given way to higher taxes, and import duties refuted his hollow promise of a chicken in every pot. Commercial markets crippled by tax and regulation reacted. Negative impact knows no home but evolves in full function affecting all.

There was a How within the Where.
The Great Depression was not a cycle, it was a resultant.
Ideology forged a void, a captured power, a nation thus controlled.

Faith and Trust had Died - Apathy the cause.
Black Friday in November 1929.
FDR waiting in the wings –

As *my tale has now come full cycle, it was January of 1932; the year I entered High School that FDR began his regime – where this tale too began.*

This text relates to a time and a maturing guy within an ever-shifting condition and an environment in flex. The narrative in generalities could portray, not in contrast but in common, the transitioning of many others. The instant test is not the finality of victory or defeat but the challenge of tomorrow. It is an individual that succeeds or fails; the result awaits a distant future day. " "We the People"" of generations past sacrificed and died as now we too control our destiny. Our constitution, the reality of our nation, is under siege – the ambitions of self-anointed elite are the termites of deceit. The confiscation of "all men are created equal" and "unalienable rights endowed" the golden goal.

Eternal vigilance our price to pay.

CHAPTER TWENTY

WHERE DO WE GO FROM HERE?

January 1932 is where and when this narration began. His demise in 1945 marked a pseudo dictatorship that many feared would never end. The resilience, the greatness of the nation was never better shown.

Ideals neither fade nor die but passing time will tarnish truth and corrode reality as fickle fate forgets. The forte, the fortitude, the precepts entwined in the founding of the nation too soon ignored. The heroism of many betrayed as lesser men in subterfuge had seized control.

Three separate and distinct branches with vested powers had lost function, the pride in stewardship and the exercise of cross disciple a fading honor no longer known. Franklin Roosevelt served four terms, the longest serving president in the nation's history. This longevity and the nature of the times fostered a governing through judicial fiat what could not be achieved under legislative procedure. Bureaucracy was not invented then but it was there and then that the appointed, the unelected, had captured stature and power. The ever-increasing power of an ever-expanding bureaucracy, the ACLU, the SEIU (Service Employees International Union), NEA (National Education Association), teachers and other unions, extremist groups of differing persuasions are a constant challenge. Ten presidents have been elected subsequent to the reign of FDR. The nation has known change, a shifting sense of value.

Harry Truman, a career senator from Missouri, also the home state of Democrat Chairman Bob Hannegan, assumed the office at the death of FDR, who by habit of intent held vice-presidents in contempt. Shielded from the presidential function and held ignorant, the deliberate intent of the one he now succeeded, Truman rose to the responsibilities. He was a converted politician now humbled in the task and completely dedicated to the office that he occupied in the whim of fate. He was unexpectedly elected to a full tern in the election of 1948.

Truman was never popular in the inner circles of intrigue and no favorite of the press. Blunt speech and simple tastes cloaked his influence and power. Denied a commanding presence, he radiated sincerity honesty and a warm down-home charm. Prompt and decisive decisions and a firm consistency bred confidence. The nation follcwed, it was not essential that they always believe. Widely respected, rarely honored, never loved, always aware of where he led. Truth and commitment what he always owned – never all alone; six years of mandatory decision of permanence in human impact – around the world. Raw courage the demand – a conscience to assuage the decision to drop the atom bomb. War was shortened, human life conserved and the potentials of nuclear energy disclosed.

The unconditional surrender of Japan and a form of governing placidly imposed. The Marshal Plan salvaged Germany as a server of the recovery in post-war Europe. Implemented the GI Bill of Rights, endured the petulance, contempt and ill temper imposed on what scme considered a substitute Commander in Chief – not qualified for military command. The jealousies of the commanders in Europe and the Pacific were separately incurred and separately endured.

General Douglas McArthur, professionally engaged in the Korean battles, referred to Eisenhower as an average clerk in his shifting corps of junior officers. Eisenhower recalled McArthur as his former instructor in theatrics. Both were suspected of political ambition, neither held the president in high personal regard or extended effort to conceal.

McArthur, testing tolerance and patience too far, was relieved of command. Eisenhower, correctly judging the electorate attitude of Democrat fatigue, was elected president as a lately identified Republican in 1952.

The Truman tenure was the end of the era of the Roosevelts. It was a fitting climax to the period of rebirth, the reincarnation born in the Civil War, then bracketed by the Japanese surrender. The end of World War II and the Chinese resurrection; the impetuous interjection of a policy of lasting presence in the far Pacific had lasting consequence.

Eisenhower, basking in the prosperity of delayed demand for luxuries denied in the lengthy war, served two terms. Military logistics was his passion, the interstate highway network, which has served so well, was the product of this initiative. A sprawling nation divided by mountain ranges and broad rivers could now be traversed from border to border and coast to coast, totally financed through a federal tax on gasoline.

Political expediency prompted the appointment of Earl Warren to the Supreme Court. The Warren court expanded and encouraged a new era of judicial activism and social disorder. Eisenhower was to later admit that the Warren appointment was his mistake.

John Kennedy, a young, articulate Democrat – the first Roman Catholic to achieve the office – was elected President in 1960. The nation was refreshed, his prompt and decisive response to Russian overtures resolved what could have developed into a true Cuban Missile Crisis. The descendent of well-reputed leaders in Boston Democrat politics, he was of the northeastern political arena but not an elitist. Assassinated before he had opportunity to mature in office, his death was a national tragedy from which some say the nation never recovered.

Lyndon Johnson assumed the office he had coveted so long. Loudly proclaiming his intentions to exploit the opportunity, he dominated the political scene. A self-termed War on Poverty was declared. A culture of dependency was created. Johnson was elected to a full term in 1962. Engulfed in the increasingly unpopular Viet Nam War, he did not seek further office, a would-be Progressive at heart, the movement and the Democratic Party merged.

It was in the Johnson tenure that federal employees were first allowed to unionize. The Social Security trust was merged with general revenue and the program immersed in the budgetary trap. It was in his term of office that efforts to prohibit the word "God" in the public square. Johnson retired, a political animal, the presidency not well served.

Richard Nixon, vice-president in the Eisenhower administration and narrowly defeated by Kennedy in 1960, was elected president in 1968 and re-elected to a shortened second term; he was the first United States President to resign the office. Overlooked in the scandals and failures in his second term is the liberal agenda of his tenure. Environmental extremism found a receptive home: Wet Lands, Endangered Species, Clean Waters, Affirmative Action among the many zip topics in vogue. Not recognized at the time were the full economic impacts that were associated with restrictions being imposed. It was then that the de-industrialization of the nation began.

Imperial attitudes prevailed and dictatorship was the title

in his fondest dreams. Gerald Ford was Nixon's Vice-President when Spiro Agnew, who was elected to the office, was forced to resign. Ford assumed the presidency at Nixon's forced departure. Ford, an honest, multi-termed Michigan Congressman, was never in full command of the office that he ascended to through appointment and default. The early presidential pardon of Richard Nixon was his most remembered act. He was defeated in his bid for a full term.

Jimmy Carter, a Naval Academy graduate and ex-governor of Georgia, was elected in 1956 on the fact that he was not the one who pardoned Richard Nixon. His administration was a disaster; the defense structure of the nation was destroyed. The American Embassy compound in Iran was invaded and the embassy staff was held hostage throughout the remainder of his term. Interest rates were in the double digits as inflation roared as he wasted billions of national wealth in quest of a synthetic alternative to gasoline. He was defeated in his pursuit of a second term.

Ronald Reagan, a two-term president, was first elected in 1980. A former actor and television personality, he had served as governor of California. He was a dynamic personality, blessed with communication skills. "That shining city on the hill" was his definition of the nation and he was believed. The nation was inspired again. The Iranian hostages were released as he took the oath of office. Demand economic policies brought prosperity and a rapid defense buildup restored national honor. An aggressive foreign policy restored confidence in military commitments. The nation again knew respect and what it is to be proud. Term limited, he had served the nation well.

George Bush, his vice-president was elected to the presidency in 1968. His most impressive resume of public service spanned his adult life. An elitist by birth he was a loosely termed closet Progressive. He publicly avowed a more kind and gentle policy than the successful course that Reagan had pursued. His solemn pledge of "No New Taxes" was betrayed in concession to a fickle Democrat Senate majority. The accomplishment of his single term in office was the demonstration of national military might. Kuwait, an Arabian ally, was invaded by Iraq and the United States responded. Iraq was occupied by U. S. forces in a few short days. Full occupation and surrender was not in the national interest. Ground forces withdrew but flight oversight was maintained for many months that followed.

William Clinton, a former governor of Arkansas, was first elected in 1988. He served two terms. His first term featured an elaborate Health Care program, which was not well received. His well-cloaked tax increase was maybe tolerated but the House of Representatives fell under a Republican majority for the first time in the memory of many. Newton Leroy "Newt" Gingrich, a dynamic leader, was to mold the good fortune. His "Contract with America" bred confidence and the President intelligently participated. A budget surplus was achieved to the credit of both. Clinton became involved in moral turpitude, was impeached by the House but not found guilty of impeachable offense by the Senate. He completed his elected term, but was again stained through his grant of presidential pardons that were of suspect.

George W. Bush, a former governor of Texas, served two terms. The son of the forty-first president was very popular, having reacted superbly to the destruction and loss of life in the World Trade Center disaster. The Tax Program that bears his name brought extended prosperity. The decision, as approved by Congress, to invade Iraq proved more costly and extended much longer than anticipated. His popularity faded.

CHAPTER TWENTY ONE

THE WORLD ~ THAT'S JUST WHERE WE LIVE

Reality, that distant beacon that attracts and then entombs what was once thought to be real. Honor the bible as the proper recording of the changing norms as man atoned yet transgressing anew. Withstanding it all was somehow decreed that man would advance in knowledge but belief and trust was left to be achieved by the individual alone.

By word apart the physical sense of being, philosophies of life, trace these transition as the icons of the sciences and doctors of the word exposed the void. There were periods of enlightenment when virtue was defined and the universe was first acclaimed. The bible forecast the coming of the Messiah in redemption but there were contrary views and those of doubt. The birth of Jesus Christ marked the distinct divisions that occurred – the state of man, as we know it now.

A new testament was added to the bible in description of departure from the Torah inherent in Christian beliefs and the year of Christ's birth identifies year one. Numbered theologies have arisen within the Christian belief. Alternate concepts of exacting devotion are in vogue and sincere practice as are those of questioned doubt or active disbelief.

However, these years of test and turmoil the mysteries of the stars were limited to the Northern Star that did not move. The passage of the sun was viewed as the passing of night to day. There were those that thought beyond but they were viewed with suspicious eye. The world was then known to be flat and to venture too far was to just disappear. It was greed for riches of the east that fractured the crust of ignorance not a quest for truth or pursuit of knowledge. It was the cunning of a queen and the ambitions of a Sailor that broke the bubble. Isabella of Spain and Christopher Columbus an Italian by birth a visionary by instinct who set sail on "That Ocean Blue".

The year was AD 1492.

Some three hundred years then passed as migration to the virgin land grew, half of the world expanded and assimilation rapidly developed. There was no existing government to subscribe to, everyone came from someplace else, there was no loyalty but bitter memories of oppressive regimes they had left behind. People tended to settle in familiar groups all concerned with future needs and the life dreams. It was natural that leaders arose and at such time, it would occur that a formal alignment of these growing groups would best serve mutual interest and concerns. Be ever mindful of the collective energy and dedication jointly shared. From this base a nation formed.

"A Nation of Virtue" in the collective absolutes and the imperatives of the word;

…One Nation Under God…
…All Men Are Created Equal…
…Endowed By Their Creator…
…Unalienable Rights…

No Nation in the history of organized control had been presented the opportunity to form a government not inhibited with already settled rules and regulations. No flamboyant leader;

"With a firm reliance on the protection of divine providence, we mutually pledge to each other
our lives, our fortunes and our sacred honor."

This solemn declaration, the severance of all ties predicated the formal establishment of governing disciplines in place of the now deficient Articles of Confederation.

The Constitution of The United States, a document of "We the People" governing under consent of the governed, rights of the individual reserved and the central authority defined:
A form, of Government unique
– "Exceptionality" – defined.

An Infant Nation was soon tested, the United States Marines delivered the nation's prompt response on the shores of Tripoli. The Monroe Doctrine proclaimed the nations sphere of protective concern. This foreign policy served well as the Nation grew. World conditions were the result of many Wars. This Nation became expensively and questionably involved in two. It was World War Two of lasting consequence in the nation's conduct of world affairs.

The United Nations was naively located here when it could have served this nation and the announced objectives better in a more neutral, less committed site. The Western Hemisphere best satisfies this goal. One of the larger islands in the Caribbean, any of the countries of Central America, or a combination of same, or Mexico would have enhanced the areas and substantively aided their economies.

Most significantly, the exceptionality of this nation's precepts of individual rights does not blend with those of contradiction. The attitudes and action so often demonstrated prompt suggestion for our declining active participation.

All three of our scheduled ambassadors to the United Nations should be promptly appointed. Their calling cards should contain the implicit message.

"From the Halls of Montezuma to the shores of Tripoli,
we guard our nations honor on land and on the sea."

CHAPTER TWENTY TWO

THIS IS WHERE WE ARE NOW

*"Where we are is always the product of that near yesterday. The truth of where we are
is not a contrast but a pragmatic, not an appraisal but a text of factual reality ."**

*I quote an ancient proverb or maybe it is one of mine.
'" "We the People"" is the academic,
Exceptionality is the distinction,
Ideology conflict is what is real.

The battle is internal; there is a rare cadre of elitists who are dedicated to a "One World Order" to which the United States Constitution disallows. There are no rules of engagement, the revolt has not been in open warfare but captivated outcomes are now the law of the land. Not to iterate but to stress the transition elements of where we are.

The Declaration of Independence and the Constitution.

The Civil War made the nation whole. Be ever aware that it took another century to finally assure voting rights to those allegedly freed. The maneuvering interlude, that era bracketed by the two President Roosevelt's, some forty years of corrupted value, not productive change. The nation emerged a world power but disruption lurked within.

Be mindful of the significance of certain presidents and the peculiarities of the times in which they served. Lincoln and Kennedy met violent ends – Wilson and FDR expired in natural demise, Nixon in resignation.

The Eighty Years of the Cold War consumed some forty-odd police actions, the USA at watch around the world. Two major wars, no victory to claim. Terrorism is a condition some still deny. There is the UN and NATO. Where are the human and fiscal resources of the nation being properly applied? Terrorism threatens. Is this dedicated threat to be aggressively defended or just foolishly denied to exist? Are policies of apology intended to replace all measures of security?

Throughout those years of turmoil the populace was overwhelmed in the challenges of poverty and prosperity. Politics and procedures knew apathy as Progressive intrigue prevailed. Ecology, environment, animal rights and entitlements dominated the political mystical square. Recall two wars were fought on foreign soil, the American public convinced by their leaders that the noble cause was the safety of democracy. That magic cause no country in Europe ever really knew but the word was in common banter. The parliamentary government of England rendered the term moot.

The Cold War was the outgrowth of World War II and blanketed the so-called free world for some forty years. Seven of the ten presidents who succeeded FDR participated in this era of contested Communistic expansion. It was the energy and foresight of the Reagan administrations that reinvigorated the nation. Communism was curtailed and economic prosperity resumed. The Korean and Viet Nam conflicts will long be debated.

The new century featured the inauguration of the forty-third president. George W. Bush lost the popular vote but gained an Electoral College majority.

The horrors of terrorism and the cost in human suffering will forever burn in the fires of memory. The character of the nation and the leadership of George Bush are legend. The incentive of low tax policies that he fostered serves so well. The invasion of Iraq consumed all energy.

The second term of George W. Bush blends with the administration to follow. The mid-term election resulted in a Democratic majority in the House. The former minority leader was elevated to speaker, a level beyond her ability to perform. Her opening address to the now minority was, "There was an election and we won." The new committee chairman mimicked, the bipartisan attitude prevailed. The two party nominations and then the campaign for the coming presidential election consumed most of the last months of the term.

The near collapse of the financial system mandated the immediate infusion of public funds to stabilize the liquidity demand of orderly commercial flow. A two-hundred-billion dollar fund was stipulated. This sizable commitment of national treasury was equality-endorsed, interest-bearing, short-term loans to financial institutions so actively engaged. The secretary of the treasury was designated as the sole controller of the fund. This designation of a single authority was unique, probably unconstitutional. Impressed with the urgency of the matter, the Congress approved the act. Both presidential candidates as sitting senators gave at least their tacit approval. Within weeks the treasury secretary determined that the credit markets were equally handicapped and, under the authority that had been granted, he diverted funding to also salvage the credit markets.

These actions all transpired with the presidential elections intervening; the treasury secretary was now serving in a lame duck capacity and his replacement was not yet appointed. The saga did not so end. The fund was substantially repaid in advance of schedule with appropriate interest but the funding was not returned to the national treasury. It was diverted to the public debt and employed in the bailout of General Motors and Chrysler in lieu of their bankruptcy.

The history of the actions, the alternates of cause, and the resultant is the topic of many studies and reports that more properly analyze than further discourse here.

The returning thrust of the Democrat nominating procedures advocated the Progressive policies of the Wilson administration in the 1920's would be remiss. The constant vow of change without definition of what it was to be was a harmonizing tune – the Hillary/Obama trademark.

Autocracy is the yield of apathy. Arrogance expands the role. There was no yearning to satisfy just created vacuums to fill. The intended confiscation of rights was not proclaimed but such power is the heart and soul the avowed intent of the Progressive Movement. The omnipotent state, the ruling ideal of all the failing powers in politically fumbling Europe versus the Constitution of the United States – rights endowed individually to man by his creator, nature's law and nature's God.

The retiring administration tolerated the sins of uncontrolled spending, derelict in the exercise of merited veto. A legacy defined in a simple phrase "the nation was kept safe – domestic needs neglected." The financial condition of the nation merits first address. The impact of incurred liabilities and forces beyond control must be acknowledged if legitimate budgeting is to be attempted.

The national debt claims an interest burden; a deficit in an annual budget or a deficiency in scheduled revenue adds to the national debt and the burden to sustain. Suppositions suggesting a full liquidation of the national debt are fantasy. This interest burden accrues from actions (might be sins) of the past. Honesty in the budgetary process demands accuracy in the forecast of interest rates and revenue anticipations. Deficit is the anticipated variance of revenue versus outlay. This difference in turn accrues to the national debt. Should the deficit in this current year aggregate $1.0 trillion and the national debt then be $10.0 trillion, the interest burden increase in ensuring fiscal years would reflect a 10% increase in this one year of the 239 odd-year history of the Republic.

Spending is the favorite target of fiscal control but elements must be separated to be attacked. The heavy increase in federal payrolls in the last ten years is pointed for concern. The staffing versus designated responsibilities should be addressed. The more recently assigned cabinet departments of Education and Homeland Security are suggested for early assignment.

These departments, still struggling for maturity, wander far and seemingly uncontrolled. Be aware that cabinets are within the scope of the Executive Branch but in reality are the black belts of operation. They are upper level appointments at the advice and consent of Congress. Bureaucracy is that unelected cadre that wields the power of implementation of acts and laws.

Aligned in theory to the Executive Branch, convenience has been served in sacrifice of ethics. Clandestine relations with some equally motivated segments of the legislative body are cancerous. Patriotism is the product of an idealism that has survived the tests of time and past challenge. The prelude of the Constitution in couple with the Declaration of Independence avow the ideal in principle and precept.

Separated powers is the instrument of disciple and function in the Constitution. The oath of office pledges individual compliance.

Elected
November 2008 AD
Current Fiscal Year Deficit
$400,000,000

Single Party Government
The President
The Speaker of the House
Senate Majority Leader

The emotions and the euphoria of election night ended all too soon. That polished veneer of humility - Now brash contempt unveiled. Raw arrogance prevails.

Inaugurated
January 20, 2009

July 30, 2009 Current Fiscal Year Deficit
(+) $1,230,000,000

Lagging Tax Receipts Suggest
Revenue Shortfall/Deficit Increase

The King/President was soon fully engulfed in the Bail Out process. In contempt or ignorant of applicable legal restrictions, he boldly proceeded to convert loans to equity via voting rights preferred stock. Administrative control of AIG, General Motors and Chrysler was questionably confiscated. Structured bankruptcy was enforced, bond holders were ruthlessly condemned.

The Majority Leader's claim of high integrity, pride in his success and a rough, tough background was betrayed in scandal. He was accused of using campaign funds to give bonuses to the doormen in his building. The charges somehow faded; "his building" was better known as the Ritz Carlton. Only a Democrat leader could get away with living at the Ritz – other politicians could not withstand the scrutiny. The leader feels the strain of re-election, being left of the Nevada center is similar to the former leader who was retired – being just left of the South Dakota Center. The Speaker represents a liberal district, re-election; considered to be sure. Her leadership, however, is dependent on a continuing majority.

Well rehearsed, local committee chairmen sponsor legislation they do not fully comprehend. The dogmatic "Princess Nancy," speaker of the house, controls all. Those hoping to survive the next election vote the party line. Constituency interests in the "Peoples House" are but secondary, elected representatives are mustered to vote "Yea" on measures that they had not been given time to read. Authorship of some of these measures has been traced to advocacy groups or registered lobbyists. Constructive suggestions from experienced sources are ignored. Such instances suggest that some also serve as indentured agents of special interests. "There was an election and we won."

Unfunded liabilities cannot be continually ignored. The additive element in this regard in the rapidly expanding bureaucracy must be attended. It is remarked that the burden of the expanded national debt that will accrue in the catastrophic result of planned annual budget differences will result in an annual debt burden in the early 2020s that is higher than the national budget total in the 1980s. The gross domestic product to off-set the burden of such off-balance is in the realm of probable inflation.

The infusion of public funds to offset decline in asset value and retarded cash flow, as currently enacted, has exploded in multiples of the projected trillion-dollar fiscal year deficit. An Economic Stimulation Package of unknown authorship, has adding some thee-hundred-million dollars, further aggravates the issue.

A misguided Carbon Cap and Trade Act that will impose destructive burdens on all working Americans is the product of activist cults and a sadly uninformed House of Representatives. Fortunately, this catastrophic legislation is on hold in the

Senate. The earth-warming topic is a United Nations adventure in Third World domination in a phantom global social order, pragmatically an adulterous fiction in the counterfeit of science and economic destruction of successful nations.

Speculative science and factual science in academic terms, separate and distinct, each awarded appropriate respect within such spectrum. Earth-warming digest and interpolation remain conjecture pending an exacting – not speculative – standard of variance. The integrity of infrastructure and input data employed in a computer modeling and interpretive technique is highly suspect. Responsible conclusions can not be the output product.

Carbon dioxide as a by-product of energy generation is a reality as is the probable contamination of ambient atmosphere. As viewed in the disciplines of Cosmology Science, the potential destruction of planet Earth is viewed as unqualified presumption. Full attention to the elimination of human hazards in proper context is in order.

The impact of expanded social programs now in debate substantially increases entitlement expense and further inflates the projected deficit. International monetary disciplines and bond rating agencies will soon dictate that an offset of the cosmetic semblance of fiscal stability is mandatory. The projected rate of increase in the national debt as today determined is threatened by negative economic forces – a decline in domestic product and lessened tax receipts portray a debt too high – risk too great – uncontrolled inflation. The catastrophic potential of a fragile debt-to-product ratio is a collapse in confidence – the true value of the United States dollar. Present convenience served at the economic destruction of future generations is the absolute of social decay – betrayal of the legacy we inherited – abandonment of moral principle.

Some 35 czars or regulators (a new level of bureaucracy) have been appointed to the presidential staff – it is expected that each will require personnel support. It is possible, if not probable, that the presidential staff could double. It has been announced that some 10,000 civil service slots have been added to cabinet departments.

The specter of a shadow government hovers in the unheralded creation of a Board of Czars. It suggests a new level of administration superseding cabinet departments and secretaries confirmed with Senatorial consent. The authority, function, staffing, logistics and designated funding of these announced operations have not been publicly disclosed.

Intimidation is the defeat of justice; too many are so victimized. Tax exempt, public funded advocacy groups allege violations. The costs to defend the threatened legal action exceeds financial resources surrender to the alternative. This type of case falsely exploits the Federal Government effectively subsidizing such action under the terms of The Civil Rights Attorney Fee Award Act of 1976. Under this act anyone who brings an even partially successful Civil Rights suit may have the defendant pay all the legal fees of both parties. This is a discretionary award routinely granted to the successful plaintiff. Successful defendants are not allowed fee reversals. This law may be right to help those who cannot afford to pursue a civil right or who may have been treated unfairly, but it has been applied to establishment clause cases unlike other civil rights litigation where someone has been denied a job or treated unfairly. There are no actionable injuries in establishment clause cases. Rich and powerful groups and organizations have exploited this advantage to enforce their ideology. When faced with the legal fees in defense and the added risk of plaintiff's legal fee liability, computed at the attorneys' hourly rate appropriate to the region – valor capitulates. Note that salaried staff or volunteer attorneys act in behalf of plaintiffs but discretionary award is computed at the regional standard attorney hourly rate; a tax-supported bonus thus too often accrues to rich and powerful advocacy groups.

Judicial Activism – that ever looming threat the
scourge of civilizations past, the seed of
first concern as this nation was conceived.

Judicial Supremacy - today again, the threat is real.
Redefining the role of God as the fundamental in our

founding is a tyranny we confront. A high and ugly wall to divide God from His people and separate historic America from the America they seek to create pollutes the scene. Elitist judges breed countless dangers; the most flagrant is continuing effort to drive God out of public life. This is in conflict with our traditions and how "We the People" choose to live our lives. That we are endowed by our Creator with unalienable rights – life, liberty and pursuit of happiness is central to our unique precepts and purpose as a nation. Our rights are the gift of God – we could not eradicate them even if we tried. Legitimacy ceases for any government that so attempts. Reflect on the wisdom of the Founding Fathers; they had a firm conviction that the purpose of government was the protection of liberty and that this purpose depended on the virtue of its citizens, thus, religion was of great benefit to society. Washington's Farewell Address best explains these sentiments. "Of all the dispositions and habits which lead to political prosperity; religion and morality are indispensable supports." Washington's words are as true today.

The Courts should recognize that the benefits of these indispensable supports that accrue to Americans not of one faith, but of all faiths and all people of good will – be they religious – or not.

Since Cooper vs. Aaron, some half-century past, the Supreme Courts have operated under the false assertion that the federal judiciary alone is supreme in the exposition of the Constitution. The single purpose in creating three branches of government was to insure "Power in the Peoples Hands" and to protect the people from any single branch having power to dictate. The doctrine of Judicial Supremacy does not exist within the Constitution.

Citizens – It is Your Call Now -
Contest this Challenge from Within.

Big Government tells Citizens What To Do.

The Constitution tells Government What It Can Not Do.

In God We Trust

CHAPTER TWENTY THREE

WHAT DO WE DO NOW?

Look first within ourselves, the luxury of citizenship claims responsibility, apathy has allowed corruptive force that only the electorate can combat. The dedication to principle and laws as constitutionally committed has been adulterated. The cult of royal rule is an ideology of despair. When in the course of human events it behooves "We the People" to remind the powers of the earth of the separate and equal status, to which the laws of nature and nature's God entitle them, there is no reminder but to recall:

The Constitution
We the People in order to form a more perfect Union...
do ordain and establish this
Constitution of the United States.

The Oath of Office
"I do solemnly swear or affirm that I will faithfully execute the
office of the president of the United States, and will to
the best of my ability, preserve, protect
and defend the Constitution of the United States."

This pledge in some similar and equal forms is the commitment of performance freely taken by all, either elected or appointed to the public trust. The theft of time and degraded attitude has scarred integrity of the oath to such positions of responsibility and commitment.

"We the People" have been betrayed in the crumbled structure and convoluted performance of both elected and appointed functionaries in the public service. This charge applies to all as their public actions or private conscience will indict.

The responsibility of stewardship that is implied in vested power has been ignored. Exercise of prerogative of action of either or both of the separate-but-equal branches of our government to react to errant action of another branch of the three is too long delinquent.

It is in order to recall the temper of that period in the Roaring Twenties that elitists so fondly refer to as their epitome. Constitutional amendments ratified within this period substantially altered the elective procedures of Article I. It modified and diminished the rural Congressional districts and converted the structure of the Congress from two interactive, interdependent legislative bodies. The disciplines of function inherent in the two senators from each state chosen by the legislature thereof.

Amendment 17 diminished the coupling of the state legislature to the Senate "Senators elected by the people" assured that the concentrated voting majorities in Urban centers would control. Senators soon assumed the posture of the upper house. The dispatch of the serious responsibilities of "Advice and Consent" and "Oversight" that are peculiar to the Senate await serious evaluation. The crumbling of separate and equal and the cross disciplines entailed was accelerated here.

Not to mention the leadership deficiencies of cabinet committee chairmen and legislative body leaders is a catastrophe of seniority. Presidents are limited to two terms in office; senators too should be so limited. Chairpersons in the House should be likewise so limited.

Amendment 16 codified the power to tax with the power to appropriate to the House of Representatives. "The Congress shall have power to lay and collect taxes on the incomes." A six-thousand page Internal Revenue Code bears witness. Numerous studies debate the obvious replacement needed. The power to tax is the power to destroy.

Not to mention the creation of the lobby industry that has arisen for the main purpose of tax code indulgence and the actual preparation of legislative detail, some of which may not even be read before enacted.

It is again in order to further to recall the temper of judicial activism that found root in the New Deal, nurtured in the Warren courts of the Eisenhower days, and has assumed a perpetuated way of life. The implementation of restrictions or actions that would not clear legislative disciplines is an invasion of rights. The Senate is reminded of prerogative of establishment of inferior courts. The instigative action is a further demand.

The Bill of Rights, Amendments 1 through 10, the absolute restriction of federal power. The first address "Congress shall make no law respecting an establishment of religion, or prohibiting the free exercise thereof." The word "religion" incorporates all theologies, all "isms," the right to believe or not believe. An errant judiciary has incorporated the phrase "Separation of Church and State." Within this invented context, the public school system has experienced catastrophic impact and the freedoms of the public square have been falsely impaired as a listless Congress has neglected to clarify.

Religious persecution is the predicate of our founding; this is a Christian nation grounded in the Judeo-Christian ideal. God is the admonition of belief as so defined. Like expressions, such as Allah, Buddha would relate to other theologies or beliefs.

Anti-Christian extremists have seized the opportunity to harass and endeavor to destroy through the file of promiscuous legal actions; fringe groups have organized actions to molest and require expenditure to resist.

Public education has been disrupted and the ambiance of public facilities attacked. The ACLU has made it their common practice to intimidate local school boards and aldermanic boards of suburban municipalities with threatened legal action should they not comply with their conception of the word God. Faced with the polluted resources of the contra-cult and the sad inadequacy of their capabilities to resist, morality and character may fade but cannot die. Not to mention that the studied intrusion into religious practice and the early contingents of the educational system is the first goal in the "ism" manifesto.

Where Best to Start?

"We the People" - Remember first just who we are and the heritage so we have so bitterly achieved. Cherish this tradition as you proudly remind the World of the beneficence, the concerns, that have been long demonstrated as an equally proud tradition, the character of this Nation. Be ever mindful of the jealousy of others, the honor to be defended and the treachery to be destroyed. Be alert to all concerns, the more certain dangers might lurk within.

Political expediency and false value has infected certain of those that have been elected to high public office, appeasement has submerged the will to resist, honor has been selectively sacrificed to hypocrisy and hollow ideal. I leave to the conjecture of others the illogical abandon of the Nation's southern border. The mantels of leadership and malfeasance of the State, Justice and Home Security Cabinet Departments, as a minimum, and impeachable delinquency in the function of Congressional oversight is alleged.

As an encompassing example, refer to the staged appearance of the President of Mexico when afforded the rare privilege to address a joint session of the Congress of the United States openly insulted the National decorum and posed the effrontery of a condescending superior.

The rousing cheer of a limited number of the assembled body that complimented this arrogance was most humiliating shock that will live in the archives of the disgraced.

Not to pay full and proper honor to those that serve with valor and those of past sacrifice in foreign lands would be remiss. I find it difficult to comprehend why drug cartels and terrorists are not judged the most vicious terrorists of all?

The expanding bureaucracy, the universe of staffs,

cabinet detainments, Congressional Committees, individual senators and representatives staff, governmental agencies and the multitude of enforcement, service, security and various separately funded activities are spiralling our national debt.

Not to mention that the average compensation of federal employees exceeds those of similar status in the private sector by a substantial margin. Federal employees are afforded the security of rival service, federal guide rules and political advantage. This not withstanding, some forty-odd percent of these federal employees are dues-paying members of the Service Employees International Union (SEIU).

The SEIU lavishly subsidizes the political infrastructure of those sympathetic to their agenda. It may be redundancy to question dedication, why a Union of Internationals can faithfully represent what is properly expected to be domestic disciplines. The governing policies, precepts and commitment are unique and exceptional in function; loyalty of those who serve is a demand.

The Department of Education in form and function is the classic misappropriation of resources and misapplication of energy and resolve. The federal government has a proper place and function in the literacy of the nation t0o ensure that "No citizen is left behind" as to equal access and opportunity to achieve the basic capabilities of communication in the English language.

All states are not economically equivalent; so it is proper that federal funds be dispersed on a pro rata basis to achieve a common state-to-state economic equivalence and educational opportunity. The federal government will correspondingly supply standardized tests for the study and teaching of English, civics and arithmetic, these the basics of literate citizenship, this to insure a minimum standard of endeavor in all states. Education is to remain a state responsibility and federal participation restricted to the above.

State and the above federal assistance should be dispersed to individual school districts under the same criterion. State school boards possessed the experience, resources and staffing that is not the complement of district school boards. The negotiations of teacher and other professional contracts and threatened legal action can best be conducted under such capacity. The wild reputation of gypsy school superintendents, the swing-door periods and exorbitant salaries paid to too many is at the denial of classroom needs. State school board participation in such activity is encouraged.

It is in order to remember that the disbursement of federal funds is the constant purview of the legislative branch. It is not to be delegated to the bureaucratic whim and achievement awards versus the enforcement of minimum standards.

The support of a cumbersome bureaucracy substantially in malfunction does not serve the classroom teacher or the striving student well. All composition, syntax scarce resources can and should be better allocated.

Rejection, revolt are words of action but it is best to reflect; what do we reject and why? This exceptional nation is a representative republic, not a democracy in the classic sense of the word. The Constitution is the code of rule to which all citizens, their elected representatives and those they may appoint are so obligated to preserve, protect and demand. Limited government and individual rights is the concern.

Elected representatives have failed the trust that they committed and betrayed the oath they swore; a bloated bureaucracy has developed, inferior courts have overwhelmed national integrity and fiscal stability standards have been degraded.

Apathy the Charge. We let it happen.
The fault is ours.

"Quo Vadis"
Where are you going?
The charge in the fading days of the Holy Roman Empire.

That haunting bugle - Blows again.
The echo being heard throughout the land.

There is no greater generation nor will there ever be one. An ever-flaming torch will be passed to whomever strives to lead and those who choose to follow. There will be times that hint of failure, tyranny cloaked in the garb of change but new leaders will arise. There will forever be that new tomorrow when that torch, the flame of "We The People," will once again ordain and establish this Constitution of the United States . . .

God Bless America

EPILOGUE

A soulful distant bugle blows "all is not well"
somewhere dwells a leader
yet to hear the call:

"We the People of the United States
in Order to form a more perfect Union..."

High school functions I deliberately avoid, the term commencement conveys a false sense of reality. Fantasy is not intended as basis of fact but as a convenient outlet to mask a divisive message veiled in an atmosphere intended to deceive.

The recent and still-grieving widow of a close friend asked if we would come with her, their daughter was the Star.

Picture that high school graduation (as though it occurs tonight) that long-awaited day that acknowledges the hurts and trials of what is now termed "Early life" and now heralds that "New beginning." Sense the emotions of the prom queen now retiring; the football captain dreams of big college offers, some others flaunt high SATs. Proud, dreary parents quietly reflect. This mystic day – nostalgia lurks ahead – transition, a secret instant never to be sensed again. Love and pride combine in defeat of time – trust and dreams to join that love - There is no between. Diaper days blend, that little girl now wears high heels, that first date – I remember waiting at a dark window for 10:30 curfew. Then faking I was just in the kitchen making coffee, I tried to hear as she and her mother giggled – I gave up – slugged a Scotch and went to bed. Confidence binds the future, "Que Sera" the song ahead. Fear – a word we knew but never felt.

Reality returns, an engulfing sunset fills the sky; this twilight belongs to those now on stage. No diploma to receive but a pass to where ambition leads. The high school principal hinted at his higher level of belief but he only likened high school to those fading days and what commencement meant as compared to the glory of the setting sun. Inspiring words, but there was something missing, no quiet pause when a cloak of unity engulfs all present in a common token to an Almighty. No opening invocation, just the ingratiating mayor thanking everyone for coming. A quiet settled in as the Valedictorian was introduced (she was someone else's daughter but could have been either one of mine).

She spoke with dignity and grace, she thanked her family, her classmates, her teachers but she had been warned not to thank her God. She spoke of her ambition in public service and requested advice and consul – she had been directed not to publicly seek guidance of the one she had by nature come to love. I felt sorrow for this daughter of another and for him too. My daughters, both just a little older, before the many-surrendered "Glory" to a few.

There was a studied pause – there was another message – suddenly she sneezed!

Her fellow graduates, as if it had been rehearsed, were on their feet, the message filled the hall as they replied in unison:

God Bless You!

The graduates had said it all.

Can one know Values

when Value knows no home.

APPENDIX

The Airplane Company was McDonnell then. Manufacturing effort was the engine cowling for the DB 7 bomber and empennage for the legendary C 47, all components of Douglas Aircraft supplied to the then United States Army. As an engineering trainee I learned there. I completed a one-week tour in tool cribs floor sweeping. I had passed the first test. I was assigned two-week tours on the burr bench and sheet metal shears/breaks. I had run into, every place I had been assigned, a guy named Wink who seemed to be delivering doughnuts from a toolbox that the guard checked only on his way out. The word was that he supervised the trucks that carried things between the company buildings around the airport. All truck drivers had jobs that paid more money. No union would accept the couple of guys that drove these inter-building trucks. The company didn't let them drive their trucks on anything that looked like a highway. My next assignment was the tech-receiving building. I was soon to learn that it was from here Wink's trucks started. My task was to help the drivers load the boxes from the Clark car-loader to the truck. It took less than a day to convince me this was the worst job they had. It was late in the morning of day two, a guy called Floyd Joe – he had a jaw full of tobacco and the foulest mouth I ever heard – backed his truck to the dock. I got on the outside end of a big box ready to help him push it on to the truck. The box was balancing on its edge as the Clark car-loader backed away. I was watching Joe across the top of the heavy box, he had a stupid grin as I sensed rather than felt him leaning into the box trying to push me off the dock. I had a higher grip than he did. I pushed back and he bounced off the side and fell on the truck floor. I pulled the box back by instinct, it settled flat. It could have fallen on top of him. I stumbled to the washroom to settle down. It only took a minute. I was walking back just as the lunch whistle had blown. Floyd Joe and two of his friends were coming toward me; they all had that stupid grin. Suddenly Wink was right beside me saying "the odds are three on two now, Floyd Baby!" All three stopped grinning as Floyd said, "Shit boss, we just wanted to teach the college son-of-a-bitch a lesson."

Before anybody had a chance to do anything I was about a foot in front of Floyd, my right fist at my side, my left finger at his throat. "You call me a son-of-a-bitch again – I'll bite your fuck'n nose off and spit it in your ugly face." Wink was shouting, "Say it again College Boy!" I was on my way back to the washroom – this time I threw up. The bastard had really tried to hurt me, I should have hit him; if Wink had not come to stand beside me, I would have.

Everybody was eating lunch when I went back. A guard was walking up the drive, cap on straight, his hand on the holstered gun, the three goons in tow. Wink passed them on the drive in the truck alone.

That afternoon, the word must have spread, guys from everywhere were happening by just to call me "College Boy." One guy did add, "You really said it all!" The "College Boy" nickname was to follow me for years.

I did not mention this incident in my weekly report. The next week the training guy took me to the main building where he introduced me to the General Foreman. The GF would tell me what was next. I didn't really care what I had been doing until he gave me the message. He was a dedicated member of the "Team," the founder was next to God and this training program was his addiction, so it was the GF's too. I had gone through the stages where many had been dropped. He would assign me to various machines and would be watching. The guys all knew I was in a program – not training for their jobs. It was up to me how much I learned. It was to be an experience that would not ever be felt again. John Bogart could mimic the first bars of the "Marine Hymn" on the Swayze Drop Hammer No. 5. Now he was perfecting "Anchors Away" on the Spence Crimper; what a guy! (I gave a talk at a management meeting about twenty years later, John was now a General Foreman – he remembered "College Boy," I remembered too. We shared a beer – it was a pitcher. I had operated the lathes, mils and a precision planer. One day the General Foreman for the first time said my name; I was to go to the Engineering Building. This was a hangar building across the field. We shook hands; "Teammates" don't say goodbye.

This is when a new life began. There were two airplanes in design the XP 67 for the Army Air Corps and the Super Secret XFD 1 for the Navy. Some ten years passed, I had become increasingly involved in probability analyses as commercially applied. I was making money as a consultant when I received an offer from a Phillco appliance distributor. Their offer dimmed the alternative of resuming a now-repetitive tour in night school to complete the credit hours toward a degree. This degree would be helpful if I were to continue in the technical arena. I took the more comfortable route; Chola and two daughters deserved the best. We moved half-way around the world when McDonnell lured me back. The SFD 1 was the first Jet Fighter in the Navy; McDonnell had first come to high-level attention through the Gargoyle, the first guided bomb to offset the publicity of Japanese suicide bombers. I was on the design team of this project.

A production contract was in view on Navy jets. Teammates keep in touch. McDonnell Aircraft was a factor. Specifications were to be agreed, formal relations had to be established with government agents. Was I interested? Two lengthy phone calls, I called collect. Two weeks later, we were on our way back home, half-way around the world. I survived many years so occupied at McDonnell.

A bit of nostalgia may fit if only to purge my mind. There was no feeling, no memories, just some things only dimly remembered, not retained.

The DC airport was not on the approved list in the first days of commercial jets. I found that I could board the TWA shuttle at 14th and K and be in Baltimore TWA Ambassadors lounge with idle time to spare. A direct jet flight would have me in St. Louis an hour before the flight from DC. I was so engaged at the hostess's desk, she would take care of the ticket, boarding pass and tell me when the Flight was boarding. The guy that had been in front of me had stopped; as I finished he turned around. After these beau coup years, Hope's dad and I just stared and shook hands. Neither said a word as we headed for the bar. "Pinch, no ice and a splash," I ordered; "No Pinch, just Chevis" was his answer as two fingers were raised. We both stared at the Scotch, neither one of us had said a word to each other. The hostess came up, gave me a boarding pass, my flight was boarding. He just gripped my arm and I gripped his. I headed for the door, neither had spoken. What was there to say? I looked back as I went out the door; he had downed his Scotch, mine still untouched. I know that was the way he left it.

He had been the closest thing to a mentor I had ever known. I wish that sometime I had given him one of my calling cards on which I had just scribbled "Thanks."

One more lonesome airplane ride, then Home.

Florida still some years ahead.

Cart mates tried to convince me that my beating up golf balls was enhancing the reputation of the group. They assured me that it was no accident, I really could find the green – I know they exaggerated, I am glad they did.

I had a choice: the clubhouse bar, or scribe this text. I hope you found a spark of interest – or maybe just a smile.

LEDGER

The Constitution – The Chronology of Construction

Virginia, the first North American colony of Great Britain.
Chartered - April 10, 1606
The British Petition of Rights - March 1628
The Charter of Massachusetts Bay Colony - March 4, 1629
The Articles of Confederation of the United Colonies of New England - September 30, 1643
The English Bill of Rights - August 1689
The Albany Plan of Union - June 30, 1754
The French and Indian Wars - 1756 - 1763
Declarations and Resolves of The First Continental Congress - October 14, 1774
Lexington "The shot heard round the world" - April 19, 1775
The Second Continental Congress/The Olive Petition to George III and his rejection of the gesture - 1775
The Declaration of Independence - July 4, 1776
The Articles of Confederation - March 1, 1781
The Paris Peace Treaty with England - 1783
United States Constitution Adopted by the Convention - September 17, 1787
Ten Amendments "The Bill of Rights" led to states ratification – 1791
"The Federalist - Anti-Federalist Papers" are honored here.
Long and detailed listing recorded elsewhere.

The Constitution Lives On

Dynamic future will record Amendments to the Constitution as they are ratified.

ABOUT THE CONTRIBUTORS

Thanks to "The American Spectator," "The Citizens Action Guide" gifted in 1996, still reminds "My Rights and Yours."

The prompt availability of fact and knowledge, free of censor, is an American asset:

The Heritage Foundation, Cato Institute, American Solutions, Think Tanks, the National Review, The Weekly Standard, Talk Radio, the Internet, and Cable Television are credited as within the essential resource of democracy.

Friends and relatives were asked to comment – their valued critiques are reflected here. They knew my boredom then; may they now know my deepest thanks.

To acknowledge is to honor all – not compare or to divide.

A nation's greatness is the virtue of those who govern and the trust of those they govern. The United States is bonded in the Constitution, a legacy of the thirteen colonies, and the forte and fortitude of our founders. There were others that helped form this nation, those who came in bondage before the nation was formed, and others who braved the hostile land alone. The persecuted and the rejected migrated here to find a life of freedom and contribute to the welfare of all. There are songs yet sung and words yet said – Naked voids – no Monuments – Forgotten – Heroes All –

They are Acknowledged Here